HOOP HYSTERIA

The College Basketball Trivia Quiz Book

**By Brent Flanders
Jeff Sigler
Randy Towner
Doug Vance**

Foreword by Roy Williams

ADDAX
PUBLISHING
GROUP

Lenexa, KS

Published by Addax Publishing Group
Copyright © 1997 by Brent Flanders and Jeff Sigler
Designed by Randy Breeden
Cover Design by Randy Breeden

Photos Courtesy: The University of Arizona, UCLA,
The University of Cincinnati, The University of Kansas,
The University of Kentucky, The University of North Carolina -
Chapel Hill, Duke University, Oklahoma State University

For information address:
Addax Publishing Group
8643 Hauser Drive, Suite 235, Lenexa, Kansas 66215

ISBN: 1-886110-28-X

Distributed to the trade by Andrews McMeel
4520 Main Street, Kansas City, Missouri 64111-7701

Printed in the United States of America

Library of Congress Cataloging - in - Publication Data

Hoop hysteria : the college basketball trivia quiz book / by Brent
Flanders ... [et al.] .
p. cm.
ISBN 1-886110-28-X
1. Basketball—United States—Miscellanea. I. Flanders, Brent E.
GV885.4.H66 1997
796.323.'63'0973—dc21 97-4095
CIP

DEDICATION

To my wife Sue and my sons Cory and Stuart, who are always there when the games are over.

– KDV

To Roy for teaching me about basketball, and to LeAnn, Libby, Katie and Abby for teaching me about everything else.

– RJT

To Suzi, Melissa and Andrew for sharing my love of college hoops, and to the memory of Dr. James Naismith, the man who started it all.

– JDS

Dedications may seem like fluff, but it is not very often that you get to thank those who have helped make you what you are. I dedicate this book and my success thus far in life to my parents, Ken and Goldie Flanders, my wife Lisa, my sons Camron and Colin, and my in-laws Richard and Jane Moore.

– BEF

A special thanks to all the sports information directors across the country who helped us on this book.

HOOP HYSTERIA/FOREWORD

By Roy Williams
Men's Basketball Coach, University of Kansas

One of the more intriguing trivia questions that you will find in this book needs further explanation. It reads something like this:

"Who is the only coach in University of Kansas history (there have been just seven) to have a losing record?"

The answer - Dr. James Naismith.

That's correct. The humble gentleman who is credited with inventing the great game of basketball at Springfield College in the winter of 1891, compiled a 55-60 career record while serving as head coach for nine seasons (1898-1907).

But I don't want that fact to tarnish the reputation of Naismith. I think it's important to understand the nature of the game in those days and the philosophy of the man who gave us the gift of basketball.

It was obviously a different game around the turn of the century. Quite often, Naismith didn't travel with his team when it made road trips. His duties on campus, whether it was leading the daily mandatory chapel services or serving as director of physical education, were much more important in his mind. When Naismith did travel with the team he was generally called upon to be the referee.

Naismith's teams didn't have a suitable on-campus court to practice or play games. The Jayhawks first home was the basement of a classroom building which had a ceiling that was a 11 feet above the floor and support posts down the middle of the court. As a result, most of the team's games were played on the road.

Naismith didn't really endorse the concept of coaching in those days. One of his star players at Kansas was a guard named Forrest C. "Phog" Allen, who enrolled at the University of Kansas in 1905. Allen made quite a name for himself as a player and attracted the attention of a nearby college. While still a player at Kansas, officials from Baker University asked Naismith if Allen could coach their team.

One afternoon Naismith called Allen into his office and said, "I've got a joke on you, you bloody beggar. They want you to coach."

"What's so funny about that?" Allen asked.

"Why, Forrest," smiled Naismith, "you can't coach basketball, you just play it."

Allen, of course, proved that basketball could be coached and Naismith later accepted that fact. Years later, Naismith presented his former pupil with a portrait with the inscription "From the Father of Basketball to the Father of Basketball Coaching."

Anyone who has walked into a gymnasium to coach, play or just watch the game of basketball since those early years owes a deep appreciation to Naismith. No one is more aware of that fact than I am.

It's interesting how coaching careers have evolved in basketball. I attended the University of North Carolina where I coached under college basketball's all-time winningest coach, Dean Smith. Coach Smith played at Kansas under Phog Allen. Allen, of course, was a product of Naismith.

When I trace the roots of my development as a coach, I'm proud to boast that the inventor of the game played a role in molding those who have influenced my career.

So when I was asked to write a forward for this book, I thought it was important to set the record straight about that one trivia question.

The game of basketball means an lot to me and countless others around the world. Its memories and traditions come alive in the pages ahead which will challenge your knowledge of basketball.

Thank you James Naismith. You started it all.

Roy Williams

USING HOOP HYSTERIA AS A GAME

In keeping with our original goal of creating a fun and exciting college basketball trivia game, we have designed this book to be played as a game! If you enjoy playing Hoop Hysteria from this book, then you'll want to order the board game using the order form at the back of this book.

Object of the Game - The object of the game is to score more points than your opponent!

Equipment - In addition to your Hoop Hysteria Trivia Book, you will need one common die, a wrist watch for a timer (optional), and a notepad and pencil (to keep score).

Beginning Play - Games are played between two teams. Teams may consist of one or more players. Teams decide before starting the game who is the home team and how the winner will be decided. Games can be played to a time limit or a preset point total, i.e., the first team to reach 100 points wins. Once these are established, a player on the visiting team tosses a coin and a player on the home team calls the toss. The winner of the coin toss is awarded possession of the die.

Playing the Game - The offense rolls the die to determine the play:

A roll of 1, 2, or 3 = Shot - If the die lands on a 1, 2, or 3, the offensive team gets the opportunity to answer a question. The defensive team opens the book randomly to a page and the offensive team chooses the question. If they answer correctly, they score the associated points. If they are incorrect, the die passes to their opponent.

A roll of 4 = Turnover - If the die lands on a 4, the offense loses possession and their opponent receives the die.

A roll of 5 = Defensive Foul - If the die lands on a 5, the offensive team gets the opportunity to answer a question as above. If they are correct, they get the point total of the question plus an additional point. If they are incorrect, they continue to have possession of the die for the next play.

A roll of 6 = Offensive Foul - If the die lands on a 6, the defensive team gets the opportunity to select the question for the offense. The defense opens the book randomly to a page and they choose a question. If the offense answers correctly the possession simply changes to the defensive team (it must have been a player-control foul!). If they answer incorrectly, the defense scores the points and receives possession of the die.

Game Format Tips - Certain rules should be decided prior to beginning play. The following are some suggestions:

• Decide what constitutes a correct answer. For example, are both first and last names required to score points? You may decide to give one point for partially-correct answers. Hoop Hysteria questions are specific in what they are asking for; trivial tidbits provided with the answer are for educational purposes and are not intended to be a part of the answer.

• Decide how much time will be given to each team to answer a question. You may use a wrist watch or some other timing device to aid you.

• Choose one player to be the scorekeeper. Only this player should be allowed to change the score.

Don't forget - if you like this book, order the official Hoop Hysteria Trivia Game today! You can find the order form at the back of this book.

CONTENTS

CHAPTER 1
ALL-AMERICANS

 1 What Brigham Young player and NBA coach was the NABC Player of the Year, Wooden award-winner, unanimous first team All-American, and academic All-American in 1981?

 2 Who was the first basketball All-American from Virginia Tech?

 3 Ed Krause, Paul Nowak, and John Moir have all been three-time consensus All-Americans. At what school did they compete?

 4 Dave Meyers was a unanimous first team all-american in 1975. At what university did Dave Meyers play?

 5 Who was the first three-time first team All-American to never appear in the NCAA tournament?

 6 What UCLA Bruin was a unanimous first team All-American, academic All-American, and the Player of the Year in college basketball in 1977?

 7 What three-time academic All-American at Maryland was on the 1972 Olympic team, helped Maryland win the NIT championship, and later became a U.S. Senator?

 8 What native of Nigeria was an All-American for Houston in 1984, while leading the nation in rebounding and field goal percentage?

 9 What 6-foot 10-inch North Carolina player was a consensus first team All-American in 1983 and 1984, having helped the Tar Heels to the 1982 NCAA title?

1 Danny Ainge

2 Dell Curry

3 Notre Dame

4 UCLA. His sister Ann was also an All-American at the same school. She later married Hall of Fame pitcher Don Drysdale.

5 Pete Maravich, of Louisiana State University

6 Marques Johnson

7 Tom McMillen

8 Hakeem Olajuwon

9 Sam Perkins

10 Who was Princeton's first All-American selection?

 11 Who is the only two-time All-American in Duquesne basketball history?

 12 Who was Mississippi State's first two-time All-American?

 13 Who was Michigan's first three-time All-American?

 14 Who are the only two consensus All-Americans in Wake Forest basketball history?

 15 Cartwright Carmichael was the first All-American in basketball at what school?

 16 What North Carolina player was on the 1976 Olympic team, a unanimous first team All-American in 1978, and won the Wooden Award in 1978?

 17 What player led the nation in scoring and rebounding in 1989, then won the Maravich Award and was a consensus second team All-American in 1990?

 18 What 7-foot 2-inch Floridian was a first team All-American in 1971 and led the nation in rebounding in 1970 and 1971?

 19 What UCLA guard was a first team All-American in 1965, was on the NCAA All-Tournament Team in 1964 and 1965 and the All-Decade Team for the sixties?

 20 What player was a first team All-American in 1980, the MOP of the 1980 tournament, and was named to the NCAA All-Decade Team for the eighties?

 21 What Bradley player was the AP's and UPI's Player of the Year, a unanimous first team All-American, on the Olympic Team, and led the nation in scoring, all in 1988?

10 Oliver deGray Vanderbilt

11 Si Green

12 Bailey Howell

13 Cazzie Russell

14 Len Chappell, who played in 1961 and 1962 and Tim Duncan in 1996 and 1997.

15 North Carolina

16 Phil Ford

17 Eric Hank Gathers

18 Artis Gilmore

19 Gail Goodrich

20 Darrell Griffith, of Louisville

21 Hersey Hawkins

Darrell Griffith

22 What West Virginia player was a unanimous first team All-American in 1959 and 1960, on the 1960 Olympic team, and on the NCAA All-Decade Team for the fifties?

 23 Who stood only 5 feet 10 inches tall and earned All-American honors while at Niagara in 1969 and 1970?

 24 Who was an All-American at Holy Cross and later went on to star with the Boston Celtics?

 25 Who was a basketball All-American at Duke in 1952 and played baseball for the Pittsburgh Pirates?

 26 What North Carolina State player was a unanimous first team All-American in 1973, 1974, and 1975?

 27 What North Carolina guard was an All-American in 1978? (Clue: you might say this at a gas station)

 28 What Georgetown player was an All-American in 1982? (Clue: don't go to sleep on this one)

 29 What 6-foot 9-inch Oklahoma player was a consensus All-American in 1983 and a unanimous all-American in 1984 and 1985?

 30 What Southwestern Louisiana player was a consensus All-American in 1972 and 1973? (Clue: his nickname was "Bo Pete")

 31 What Notre Dame player was an All-American in 1974? (Clue: he later went on to coach at S.M.U.)

 32 What Georgetown player was an All-American center in 1984?

 33 What two Loyola Marymount players were second team All-Americans in 1989-90?

 34 What Michigan player was an All-American in 1966?

 35 What Western Kentucky player was an All-American in 1967 and the NABC college coach of the year in 1997.

22 Jerry West

23 Calvin Murphy

24 Bob Cousy

25 Dick Groat

26 David Thompson

27 Phil Ford

28 Eric " Sleepy " Floyd

29 Wayman Tisdale

30 Dwight Lamar

31 John Shumate

32 Patrick Ewing

33 Bo Kimble and Hank Gathers

34 Cazzie Russell

35 Clem Haskins

David Thompson

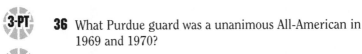

3-PT **36** What Purdue guard was a unanimous All-American in 1969 and 1970?

3-PT **37** What Indiana guard was an All-American in 1981?

3-PT **38** What 6-foot 4-inch Arkansas standout was a first team All-American in 1979 and lead the nation in field goal percentage in 1976 with a 66.5 mark?

3-PT **39** UCLA's Lew Alcindor and Bill Walton are two of the eight players to be unanimous first team All-Americans for three straight years. Name three others.

3-PT **40** Since 1970 only three players have been unanimous first team All-Americans for three straight years. Who are they?

3-PT **41** What Stanford great was a consensus All-American in 1936 and a unanimous All-American in 1937 and 1938?

3-PT **42** What Purdue standout was a consensus All-American in 1930 and a unanimous All-American in 1931 and 1932?

3-PT **43** What Oklahoma A&M center was a consensus All-American in 1944 and a unanimous All-American in 1945 and 1946?

3-PT **44** What La Salle center was a consensus All-American in 1953 and a unanimous All-American in 1954 and 1955?

3-PT **45** What Kentucky player was a unanimous All-American in 1947 and 1948 and a consensus All-American in 1949?

3-PT **46** What DePaul center was a unanimous All-American for three straight years from 1944 to 1946?

2-PT **47** What Cincinnati standout was a unanimous All-American for three straight years from 1958 to 1960?

36 Rick Mount

37 Isiah Thomas

38 Sidney Moncrief

39 Jerry Lucas, Pete Maravich, George Mikan, Oscar Robertson, Ralph Sampson, and David Thompson

40 Ralph Sampson (1981-83), David Thompson (1973-75), and Bill Walton (1972-74)

41 Hank Luisetti

42 John Wooden

43 Bob Kurland

44 Tom Gola

45 Ralph Beard

46 George Mikan

47 Oscar Robertson

Ralph Beard

48 David Greenwood was a consensus All-American in 1978 and 1979 while playing for what team?

 49 San Francisco has had two consensus All-Americans from 1950 through 1990. Bill Russell is one of them. Who is the other?

 50 Seattle had two consensus All-Americans in the 1950s. One of them was Johnny O'Brien in 1953. Who was the other?

 51 St. Bonaventure has produced two unanimous All-Americans. Name one of them.

 52 Les Witte (1932, 1934) and Ken Sailors (1943) were consensus All-Americans from what western university?

 53 Gene Englund (1941) and John Kotz (1942) were consensus All-Americans from what Big Ten school?

 54 Dave Stallworth (1964) and Xavier McDaniel (1985) were consensus All-Americans from what Missouri Valley Conference school?

 55 Price Brookfield was a unanimous All-American at what Texas school in 1942?

 56 Hal Lee (1934) and Bob Houbregs (1953) were consensus All-Americans from what PAC-10 school?

 57 What two Syracuse players were unanimous All-Americans in 1990 and 1991?

 58 What two St. John's players were named unanimous All-Americans in 1985 and 1986?

 59 Who was the first unanimous All-American for UCLA?

 60 What player became the first consensus All-American from Oregon State?

 61 Stacey King was a unanimous All-American for what school in 1989?

48 UCLA

49 Quintin Dailey, in 1982

50 Elgin Baylor, in 1958

51 Tom Stith, in 1961, and Bob Lanier, in 1970

52 Wyoming

53 Wisconsin

54 Wichita State

55 West Texas State

56 Washington

57 Derrick Coleman, in 1990, and Billy Owens, in 1991

58 Chris Mullin, in 1985, and Walter Berry, in 1986

59 Walt Hazzard, in 1964

60 Steve Johnson, in 1981

61 Oklahoma

62 Who **was the first** unanimous All-American for UNLV?

 63 At what school was Sid Tannebaum a consensus All-American in 1946 and 1947?

 64 Dean Meminger and Jim Chones were consensus All-Americans at what school in 1971 and 1972 respectively?

 65 At what Jerry Tarkanian-coached school was Ed Ratleff a unanimous All-American for two straight years?

 66 At what school was Bob Boozer a consensus All-American in 1958 and a unanimous All-American in 1959?

 67 Who was Louisville's first unanimous All-American?

 68 Forrest "Aggie" Sale was the first unanimous All-American at what university?

 69 Who was Louisiana State University's first unanimous All-American?

 70 Doug Collins was a consensus All-American at what university in 1973?

 71 Vernon Huffman, Ernie Andres, Ralph Hamilton, and Don Schlundt were consensus All-Americans at what university?

 72 What Miami player was a unanimous All-American in 1965 while leading the nation in scoring, and is in the Naismith Memorial Basketball Hall of Fame?

 73 Aggie Sale, Leroy Edwards, Bob Brannum, Cliff Hagan, Johnny Cox, and Cotton Nash were all consensus All-Americans for what university?

62 Larry Johnson, in 1991

63 New York University

64 Marquette

65 Long Beach State, in 1972 and 1973

66 Kansas State

67 Wes Unseld, in 1967

68 Kentucky, in 1932 and 1933

69 Pete Maravich, in 1968. He repeated the honor in 1969 and 1970

70 Illinois State University

71 Indiana

72 Rick Barry

73 Kentucky

Bob Boozer

CHAPTER 2
COACHES

 1 UCLA's John Wooden coached the Bruins to how many NCAA titles?

 2 Whose name adorns the trophy presented annually by the Commonwealth Athletic Club to the nation's most outstanding collegiate basketball player?

 3 Which two coaches have taken more teams to the Final Four than Louisville's Denny Crum?

 4 Which coach has won 500 games faster than any other coach?

 5 What coach took his team to its record 23rd straight NCAA tournament appearance in 1997?

 6 What legendary player coached Boston College from 1963 to 1969?

 7 What successful NBA coach was the coach of Boston College from 1969 to 1971?

 8 From 1972 to 1975, what coach led Bucknell to a 33-42 record?

 9 Lute Olson coached at two major colleges before coaching at the University of Arizona. Name one.

 10 Bobby Knight began coaching at Indiana University in 1972. At what school did he coach before Indiana?

 11 Before he retired, Johnny Orr coached at Michigan and Iowa State. Name two others schools where Johnny Orr coached.

 12 Name the all-time winningest coach at Iowa State University.

1 In John Wooden's 27 years as the UCLA head coach his teams won an unprecedented ten titles. As the Bruin coach he amassed a 620 - 147 record.

2 Adolph F. Rupp

3 John Wooden at UCLA and Dean Smith at North Carolina.

4 Jerry Tarkanian, who won his 500th in the 28th game of his 20th year of coaching while at the University of Nevada-Las Vegas.

5 Dean Smith, of North Carolina

6 Bob Cousy

7 Chuck Daly

8 Jim Valvano

9 The University of Iowa and Long Beach State

10 Army

11 Wisconsin and Massachusetts

12 Johnny Orr

Adolph F. Rupp   *John Wooden*

13 Before becoming coach at the University of South Carolina, Eddie Fogler was a head coach at what two other institutions?

 14 What legendary coach's son assumed the head coaching job at Texas Christian University during the 1987-1988 season?

 15 Who was the coach at Ball State University from 1987 to 1989?

 16 With 875 victories and 190 losses, who is the second all-time winningest coach in NCAA history?

 17 Where did University of North Carolina coach Dean Smith attend college?

 18 In 1984, who became the head basketball coach at the University of Kansas?

 19 The 1972-73 season brought a new coach to Georgetown University. Name that coach.

 20 Who became the head basketball coach at the University of Tulsa in the 1980-81 season?

 21 Who coached the 1985 national champion Villanova Wildcats?

 22 At what university did Georgetown University basketball coach John Thompson play his college basketball?

 23 NBA coaching legend Lennie Wilkins played his college basketball at what school?

 24 Who coached two seasons at Providence, compiled a 42-23 record, and took the Friars to one Final Four?

 25 On March 25, 1992, what former New York Knickerbockers NBA coach became the coach at the University of Wisconsin?

26 What did Montana State's head coach, Ott Romney, create when he was said to have concocted "racehorse basketball?"

13 Vanderbilt University and Wichita State University.

14 Moe Iba

15 Rick Majerus

16 Adolph Rupp, who coached the University of Kentucky to 41 consecutive winning seasons.

17 The University of Kansas

18 Larry Brown

19 John Thompson

20 Nolan Richardson

21 Rollie Massimino

22 Providence

23 Providence

24 Rick Pitino

25 Stu Jackson

26 The fast break.

Rick Pitino

27 Pete Newell coached what university to the 1959 NCAA championship?

28 Who coached Iona College from 1976 to 1980, compiling a 95-46 record?

29 How many Kansas University head coaches have failed to take a team to the NCAA Final Four since the inception of the NCAA Tournament?

30 Dale Brown succeeded what coach at LSU?

31 What Purdue Boilermaker was national Player of the Year in 1932 and went on to be one of the great legends in college coaching?

32 What coach compiled a 17-8 record in 1946-47 and a 27- 7 record in 1947-48 at Indiana State University, but established his coaching legend later with another school?

33 Lute Olson, Jerry Tarkanian, and Tex Winter have all been the head coach at what university?

34 From 1972 to 1981, Press Maravich and Bobby Cremins both coached at what university?

35 On March 23, 1930, what Freeport, Illinois high school coach became the head basketball coach at the University of Kentucky?

36 Who is the Wizard of Westwood?

37 Who was the first coach to guide four different schools to the NCAA tournament?

38 Ray Meyer, the DePaul coaching legend, was a star on the 1935-36 squad that won the Helms Foundation national championship. At what school did Ray Meyer play?

27 The University of California.

28 Jim Valvano

29 Dr. Forrest Allen, Dick Harp, Ted Owens, Larry Brown, and Roy Williams have all taken teams to the Final Four in their careers as head coach at Kansas.

30 Press Maravich

31 John Wooden

32 John Wooden

33 Long Beach State

34 Appalachian State

35 Adolph Rupp

36 John Wooden

37 Eddie Sutton

38 Notre Dame

Eddie Sutton

39 Robert Dowell, Gary Colson, and Jim Harrick all coached at what university?

 40 Name two UCLA players who have also coached the basketball team at UCLA.

 41 What is Bobby Cremins's alma mater?

 42 What is Denny Crum's alma mater?

 43 Before George Raveling was the coach at USC, what other Pac-10 team did he coach?

 44 Who was Naismith Coach of the Year in 1988, an Olympic coach in 1980, and an Olympic team member in 1964?

 45 Who was the coach at Army from 1966 through 1971?

 46 Who was the coach at Army from 1976 to 1980?

 47 Who has coached at Tufts, Columbia, Fordham, Rhode Island, and Texas?

 48 Coach Don Haskins is a graduate of what university?

 49 Gene Bartow has taken which two schools to the NCAA Final Four?

 50 Hugh Durham has coached which two teams in the NCAA Final Four?

 51 Jack Gardner has coached which two teams in the Final Four?

 52 Lou Hensen has coached which two teams in the NCAA Final Four?

39 Pepperdine

40 Walt Hazzard and Larry Farmer.

41 The University of South Carolina.

42 The University of California-Los Angeles.

43 Washington State

44 Larry Brown

45 Bob Knight

46 Mike Krzyzewski

47 Tom Penders

48 Oklahoma State (1953)

49 Memphis State and UCLA.

50 Florida State and Georgia.

51 Kansas State and Utah.

52 New Mexico State and Illinois.

Mike Krzyzewski   *Larry Brown*

53 Frank McGuire has coached which two teams in the NCAA Final Four?

 54 Lute Olsen has coached which two teams to the NCAA Final Four?

 55 Lee Rose has coached which two different teams in the NCAA Final Four?

 56 Who was the first coach to win back-to-back NCAA championships?

 57 Eddie Sutton has coached what four schools in the NCAA tournament?

 58 What teams has Digger Phelps coached in the NCAA tournament?

 59 Bill Frieder became the coach at Arizona State in 1990. What college did Bill Frieder coach before Arizona State?

 60 Before joining Cincinnati University, Bob Huggins coached for five seasons at what college?

 61 The great Hank Iba coached Oklahoma State in the Big Eight but also coached what other Big Eight school?

 62 The legendary Phog Allen, well-known for his 746 wins at the University of Kansas, also coached at three other universities. Name one.

 63 Although most widely known for being the coach at Oregon State, Ralph Miller also coached at two other universities. Name one.

 64 What did John Wooden always hold in his hand when he coached?

 65 Who coached Phi Slamma Jamma?

53 St. John's and North Carolina

54 Iowa and Arizona

55 North Carolina-Charlotte and Purdue

56 Henry Iba, of Oklahoma A&M in 1945 and 1946.

57 Creighton, Arkansas, Kentucky, and Oklahoma State

58 Fordham and Notre Dame

59 The University of Michigan

60 At Akron University in Ohio, from 1984 through 1989, compiling a 97-46 record.

61 Hank Iba coached at the University of Colorado before he became legendary at Oklahoma A&M (now known as Oklahoma State).

62 Baker, Haskell, and Central Missouri State. Baker is located in Baldwin, Kansas. Haskell is located in Lawrence, Kansas. Central Missouri State is located in Warrensburg, Missouri.

63 Wichita State and Iowa

64 A program

65 Guy Lewis

Henry Iba

66 Four coaches have won 100 or more games in their first four seasons as a Division I head coach. Name two.

 67 Where did Eddie Fogler begin his collegiate head coaching career?

 68 John McLendon became the first black head coach of an integrated university program in 1966. At what school did McLendon win his 500th game?

 69 Only three coaches had won 200 games at two different schools in their coaching careers. Name two.

 70 What three active coaches have won two or more national championships?

 71 Name the two North Carolina coaches who have guided their teams to national championships.

 72 Forddy Anderson and Jud Heathcote have guided what team to the NCAA championship?

 73 Three different coaches have taken Indiana to the NCAA championship game. One is Branch McCracken, another is Bob Knight. Who is the third?

 74 Three different coaches have taken Oklahoma State University to the NCAA tournament. Two of them are Henry Iba and Eddie Sutton. Name the third.

 75 What two schools has Larry Brown coached to the NCAA championship game?

 76 Cotton Fitzsimmons guided what team to the NCAA tournament?

 77 Doggie Julian took what team to the Final Four twice?

 78 Bill Foster, Vic Bubas, and Harold Bradley have all guided what team to the NCAA tournament?

66 They are Everett Case, of North Carolina State, Roy Williams, of Kansas, Jim Boeheim, of Syracuse, and Speedy Morris, of La Salle.

67 Wichita State, in 1986

68 Cleveland State

69 Hugh Durham, Ralph Miller, and Norm Sloan

70 Indiana's Bob Knight, Louisville's Denny Crum, Duke's Mike Krzyzewski

71 Frank McGuire and Dean Smith

72 Michigan State

73 Lou Watson, in 1967

74 Paul Hansen

75 UCLA and Kansas

76 Kansas State, in 1970

77 Holy Cross, in 1947 and 1948

78 Duke

Roy Williams

79 Steve Fisher coached Michigan in the 1989 NCAA tournament. Who was the coach during the regular season?

 80 On September 10, 1960, this coach became college basketball's first Triple Crown winner, having been a winning coach in the Olympics, the NCAA tournament, and the NIT.

 81 What former Villanova star and NBA coach is credited with the first three-point field goal in NBA history?

 82 Who was the first African-American coach to win the NCAA Division I championship?

 83 In what year was Bobby Knight's first trip to the Final Four?

 84 Who is the only coach to take teams to the Final Four in four different decades?

 85 In what years did Oklahoma State's Hank Iba coach the U.S. Olympic team?

 86 Who is the only coach to win a NCAA title in his first full season at a school?

 87 Who was Miami-Ohio's leading scorer when it upset defending champion Marquette in the 1978 NCAA tournament?

 88 Who is the only major college coach with more than seven hundred victories to never reach the Final Four?

 89 What is the only school to have five different coaches lead its teams to the Final Four?

 90 Who was the first coach to play for an NBA championship and to coach a NCAA champion?

91 Who was the first player to play in an NCAA championship game and later coach his alma mater in a championship game?

79 Bill Frieder

80 Pete Newell

81 Chris Ford made the first three-pointer on October 12, 1979.

82 John Thompson

83 In 1960, as a player for Ohio State University

84 Dean Smith

85 In 1964, 1968, and 1972

86 Ed Jucker, of Cincinnati

87 Randy Ayers

88 Ed Diddle, of Western Kentucky

89 Kansas

90 John Thompson, who played for the Celtics and coached Georgetown.

91 Dick Harp, at The University of Kansas, who played in the 1940 championship game against Indiana and coached the 1957 runner-up Kansas team against North Carolina.

Ed Jucker

Dick Harp and Phog Allen

3-PT **92** What coach was a backup center for Bill Russel in the NBA?

2-PT **93** Which two coaches were opposing their alma maters in the Final Four in 1991 and again in 1993?

2-PT **94** Who is the only coach to oppose his alma mater more than twice at the Final Four?

2-PT **95** Who was the first NCAA tournament Most Outstanding Player who later coached his alma mater in the tournament?

2-PT **96** Who was the first coach to see forty years pass between his first and his last appearance in the NCAA tournament?

2-PT **97** Who was the first NCAA College World Series championship coach to direct a basketball team from the same school to the Final Four?

3-PT **98** What was the first father-son combination to twice reach the Final Four together as coach and player?

2-PT **99** At what university did Caddy Works coach for eighteen seasons?

2-PT **100** Who were the first two men to have played for and coached NCAA tournament champions?

3-PT **101** What sport other than basketball did Dean Smith letter in while he was at Kansas?

3-PT **102** What school has graduated the most coaches who have taken their teams to the NCAA tournament?

2-PT **103** At what school did Mike Krzyzewski play basketball?

2-PT **104** At what school did Al McGuire play?

3-PT **105** Who became the first African-American college coach elected to the Basketball Hall of Fame?

92 John Thompson, of Georgetown

93 Roy Williams of Kansas met North Carolina's Dean Smith in the semi-finals both years.

94 Denny Crum opposed his alma mater, UCLA, in the Final Four in 1972, 1975 and 1980.

95 Walt Hazzard, of UCLA

96 Ray Meyer, of DePaul

97 Sam Barry, of Southern California

98 Houston's Guy Lewis and son Vern. Five of Guy's teams played in the NCAA Final Four, three won 31-or-more games, four won conference championships and two won the Southwest Conference Post-Season Tournament.

99 The University of California-Los Angeles

100 Bob Knight and Dean Smith

101 Baseball

102 St. Joseph's, in Pennsylvania, with eight

103 Army

104 St. John's

105 John McLendon

Denny Crum

CHAPTER 3
RULES

 1 How many rules of basketball did Dr. James Naismith originally have when he invented the game in 1891?

 2 The original game of basketball, as invented by James Naismith, had two halves. How long were they?

 3 In the original rules of basketball, what happened when a team committed three consecutive fouls?

 4 What is the width of a basketball court?

 5 What is the regulation size of a backboard?

 6 What play did the NCAA rules committee outlaw in 1967?

 7 What revolutionary change in 1938 resulted in more playing time, higher scores, and pattern offenses and defenses?

 8 Taking away some of the advantage of tall players like George Mikan and Bob Kurland, the 1944-45 season saw what new rule introduced?

 9 Dr. Naismiths's original rules of basketball allowed you how many seconds to inbound the ball?

 10 What is the length of a basketball court?

 11 What shall be parallel to the end line and have its further edge 15 feet from the plane of the face of the backboard?

 12 May a team play with fewer than five players?

1 Naismith designed the game with 13 rules. The first major change in the rules was to limit a team to five players.

2 Fifteen minutes, compared to 20 minutes today, with a 5-minute rest between each half.

3 Their opponents would be awarded a goal.

4 50 feet (which is a little over half the length of the court)

5 6 feet wide by 4 feet high

6 Forcing the ball downward through the basket, also known as the dunk.

7 The elimination of the center jump after each score.

8 The goaltending rule, which made it illegal for a player to touch the ball after it had begun its downward flight toward the basket.

9 Five seconds

10 94 feet

11 The free throw line

12 Yes, a team must begin with five players, but if it has no substitutes it may continue with fewer than five.

Dr. James Naismith

13 If the ball enters the basket from below, goes through, and drops back into the basket, is it a goal scored?

14 In 1895, the free throw line was moved to 15 feet, where it is today. How far was it originally?

15 In 1896, field goals were changed to two points. What were they changed from?

16 In 1896, free throws were changed to one point. What were they before 1896?

17 Before 1908, how many officials were there in a basketball game?

18 In 1911, how many fouls were each player permitted before fouling out?

19 In 1949, coaches were first allowed to do what during a game?

20 In 1973, NCAA bylaws were changed to allow what?

21 Excitement came back into the game in 1977 as a result of this rule change. What was it?

22 At what distance is the three-point line in college?

23 What is another word for the division line?

24 How many feet of unobstructed space do the rules call for outside the lines of the basketball court?

25 What must be two inches in width and have a radius of two feet?

26 How wide is the free throw lane?

13 No, it is a violation

14 20 feet from the end line

15 Three points

16 Three points

17 One. Because of increasingly rough play, a second official was added for the 1908-1909 season.

18 Four

19 Speak to players during a time out. We have to wonder if this rule change was welcomed by the players...

20 To allow incoming freshmen the opportunity to play varsity basketball during their freshman year.

21 The dunk was made legal after a ten year experiment in which it was a violation.

22 It is 19 feet 9 inches from the center of the basket

23 The division line is also called the half-court line or time line

24 At least 3 feet, preferably 10 feet

25 The center circle

26 12 feet

27 How many marked lane spaces are there on each side of the free throw lane?

28 What are backboards required to have on their bottom edge?

29 How many feet above the floor is the top of the backboard?

30 What is the diameter of the basket's rim?

31 This part of the basket must be 15 to 18 inches in length and suspended from beneath the rim. What is it?

32 This must be circular and 5/8 of an inch in diameter. What is it?

33 What color must the rim be?

34 How many leather panels are on a basketball?

35 Only the manufacturer's name or logo or both is permitted on this. What is it?

36 This must weigh between 20 and 22 ounces. What is it?

37 Who provides the ball for a basketball game?

38 Who decides which direction the teams will play in the first half of a college basketball game?

39 What is 28 feet long and 3 feet wide on a basketball court?

40 What color must the three-point line match?

27 Four

28 Padding

29 13 feet

30 18 inches

31 The net

32 The rim

33 Bright orange

34 Eight

35 The basketball

36 The basketball

37 The home team

38 The visiting team

39 The coaching box. How come nobody stays in it?

40 It must be the same color as the free throw lane's boundary lines

41 Who tosses the ball to start a game, the umpire or the referee?

 42 What may only be used in situations involved in preventing or rectifying a scorer's or timer's mistake or malfunctioning clocks?

 43 What must identify the school, the school's nickname or mascot, or the player's name?

 44 What is the highest number that a player can wear on his uniform?

 45 What is the lowest number that a player can wear on his uniform?

 46 What is the maximum number of colors allowed on a player's uniform number?

 47 This occurs when a player touches the ball or basket while the ball is on or in the basket or while it is within an imaginary cylinder extending up from the rim.

 48 This is illegal personal contact by pushing or moving into an opponent's torso.

 49 This is illegal personal contact that impedes the progress of an opponent.

 50 This occurs when a player gains control of a ball that is neither in the cylinder nor on the rim and then attempts to drive, to force, or stuff the ball through the basket.

 51 This occurs when two players commit personal fouls against each other at approximately the same time.

 52 What type of foul is it when no legitimate attempt has been made to play either the ball or a player?

 53 What is the term for movement of the ball caused by a player who throws, bounces, or rolls the ball to another player?

41 The referee

42 A television monitor. Of course it is also a popular devise used to watch basketball games from a point outside the arena.

43 The player's uniform

44 55. This rule was adopted during 1957-1958 to make it easier for official scorers to record personnal fouls on players–it is the highest number that can be signalled by an official using one hand with two gestures.

45 0 or 00. The number zero is indicated by an official to the official scorer by a closed fist.

46 Three

47 Basket interference

48 Charging

49 Blocking

50 Dunking

51 A double personal foul

52 An intentional foul

53 Pass

54 The definition of this term is moving one or both feet in any direction in excess of prescribed limits while holding the ball inbounds.

55 What is the score of a forfeited game?

56 Once a player is given the ball to shoot a free throw, how long does he have to shoot it?

57 When can a player leave his marked area to rebound a free throw?

58 What happens on a free throw if the ball lodges between the rim and the backboard, or comes to rest on the plate behind the rim?

59 What should happen if a scoring error is discovered in a period following the one in which the error occurred?

60 What happens during a game if you exceed your alloted number of time outs?

61 How many free throws are alloted for a technical foul?

62 What does it mean when an official places his left hand on top of his head?

63 What is an official signalling when he holds both hands above his head?

64 What is an official signalling when he brings both hands down to his hips?

65 What is an official signalling when he places his right hand behind his head?

66 What is an official signalling when he crosses both hands above his head?

67 What is a player-control foul more commonly known as?

54 Traveling

55 Two to zero. The two points are not awarded to a player.

56 10 seconds

57 Once the ball has left the shooter's hands

58 It is a violation and the ball is awarded to the other team.

59 The score should be corrected and play continued.

60 A technical foul is assessed.

61 Two

62 Shot clock violation

63 A successful three-point shot

64 A blocking foul

65 A player control foul or charge

66 An intentional foul

67 A charge

68 Why was "The Triangle," a magazine that the School for Christian Workers published on January 15, 1892, an important printed material for college basketball?

69 Beginning in 1921, what were the two sections of the court known as?

70 Before its width was changed to 12 feet in 1956, how wide was the free throw lane?

71 Beginning in the 1963-1964 season, players were made to do what after being assessed a personal foul? Clue: This may have provided a popular deodorant company with an advertising idea.

72 Can there be more than one center jump in a regulation NCAA game?

73 What change was made to the shot clock for the 1993-1994 season?

74 Were college basketball games ever played in quarters instead of halves?

75 What was the official infraction called when the NCAA began disallowing the dunk in 1967?

76 In what year did the NCAA adopt the three-point field goal?

77 In what year were rectangular glass backboards made official for college basketball? Was it 1928, 1938, 1948, or 1958?

78 When was the shot clock first introduced to college basketball? Was it 1984, 1985, or 1986?

79 What is the most number of players that can be on the court for one team at any time?

80 What does "carom" mean in basketball?

81 What does "assist" mean in basketball?

68 It was the first printing of Dr. James Naismith's 13 Original Rules of Basket ball.

69 The frontcourt and the backcourt

70 6 feet. We wonder if Bill Russell or Wilt Chamberlain had anything to do with this change?

71 Raise an arm. The rule was reversed before the 1974-1975 season although the action was encouraged.

72 Yes - If a held ball occurs after the referee tosses the ball and before a team has possession, another center jump occurs.

73 It went from 45 seconds to 35 seconds.

74 Yes, during 1951-1952 and 1952-53 the game was played in four 10-minute quarters.

75 During a game it was called offensive goaltending although dunking was also disallowed during pregame warmups.

76 1987

77 Before 1948 there wasn't an official shape for backboards.

78 The 45-second clock was introduced in 1986. A team must shoot the ball and touch the rim within 45 seconds of attaining possession of the ball.

79 Five

80 Rebound

81 A pass to a teammate which leads directly to a field goal

CHAPTER 4
I DIDN'T KNOW THAT

 1 The John Wooden Award for college basketball's player of the year is presented by what athletic club?

 2 Weeb Ewbank coached the Baltimore Colts to the NFL championship and the New York Jets to the Super Bowl championship. Where was Ewbank a basketball coach?

 3 Who is the only coach of a NCAA champion to play major league baseball?

 4 Who was the first coach to guide a team to the College World Series championship and a team to the NCAA basketball championship?

 5 What coach played in the NCAA tournament and the College World Series in 1965 for the University of Connecticut?

 6 What former Kansas basketball coach is credited with inventing the football helmet?

 7 What college basketball coach was the golf coach from 1967 until 1973 at Syracuse?

 8 What university located in Nashville, Tenn. first fielded a men's basketball team?

 9 The first basketball backboards were made of what material?

 10 In what year was basketball invented?

 11 What kind of ball was used during the first three years of basketball?

 12 How many players were on the first basketball teams in the games played at Springfield?

1 The Los Angeles Athletic Club

2 Brown University

3 Fred Taylor, of Ohio State, pitched for the Washington Senators.

4 Everett Dean, of Stanford

5 Tom Penders

6 Dr. James Naismith

7 Jim Boeheim

8 The Vanderbilt Commodores fielded the first men's team in 1893.

9 The first backboards were made of wire mesh.

10 Dr. James Naismith invented the game of basketball in the winter of 1891 in Springfield, Mass.

11 Dr. James Naismith selected a soccer ball and peach baskets were used for the goals.

12 Nine. Naismith had 18 students in his YMCA physical education class and he split the group in half.

James Naismith

13 Who is the only basketball coach with a losing record at the University of Kansas?

 14 At what height were the first peach baskets hung at the YMCA Training School in Springfield, Mass.?

 15 In what country was James Naismith, the inventor of the game of basketball, born?

 16 On February 9, 1895, Minnesota State School of Agriculture crushed Hamline College 9-3. Why was this game significant in the history of the game?

 17 In 1892, basketball began its worldwide movement. What was the first foreign country to have basketball games?

 18 In 1893, The Narragansett Machine Co. of Providence, R.I., introduced these to eliminate peach baskets.

 19 In 1894, the Overman Wheel Company became the first company to manufacture a sphere that became fundamental to the game. What was it called?

 20 What was significant about the game played on January 16, 1896, between the University of Chicago and Iowa University? (Hint: It was a change from Naismith's orignial 13 rules that is still in place today.)

 21 Who presented the Olympic medals to the winning basketball teams in the 1936 Olympics played in Berlin?

 22 Why were backboards introduced to the game of basketball?

 23 At what college did James Naismith work when he invented the game in 1891?

24 Who did James Naismith send to retrieve the apparatus for the first basketball game?

13 James Naismith, the inventor of the game, compiled a record of 55 wins and 60 losses while at Kansas. Naismith, however, didn't travel to many games and really didn't endorse the concept of coaching the game.

14 When Naismith invented the game, he had requested that the janitor bring him boxes for the targets. Instead, the janitor brought peach baskets. He fastened the baskets to either end of the gym to a track 10 feet above the floor.

15 Naismith was born in Canada. He died in 1939 at the age of 78 and is buried in Lawrence, Kansas.

16 It marked the first basketball game played between two colleges.

17 Mexico

18 It brought the first iron rims with braided cord netting to the game.

19 The company produced what we know today as a basketball.

20 It was the first college game with five players on a side.

21 Dr. James Naismith, the man who invented the game, presented the medals and witnessed the world wide growth of basketball.

22 The original goals were placed on balconies and backboards were needed to prevent fans from interfering with shots.

23 Springfield College, in Springfield, Massachusetts

24 Pop Stebbins, the janitor at the Springfield, Massachusetts YMCA, where Naismith invented the game. He brought Naismith peach baskets to use as the targets for the game.

25 If Pop Stebbins had retrieved what James Naismith had requested, what would basketball be called today?

 26 Who asked James Naismith to develop a game that could be played indoors between the football and baseball seasons?

 27 What university qualified for the NCAA tournament in 1993 thereby making its state the last to have an eligible basketball team qualify?

 28 Name the smallest Division 1 school in the nation.

 29 Mike Ditka, pro football hall-of-fame player and coach, lettered for what college basketball team?

 30 On November 29, 1980, Ronnie Carr of Western Carolina University made NCAA history by hitting the first one of these. What was it?

 31 How many schools are in the Big Ten conference?

 32 What was the name of the Big Eight conference immediately before it became the Big Eight?

 33 What is the only team to have been prevented from defending its national title due to NCAA probation?

 34 What state is represented the most in NCAA Division I basketball?

 35 The great Jackie Robinson is the only four-sport, including basketball, letter winner at what school?

 36 What collegiate basketball great has been on the cover of Sports Illustrated 27 times?

 37 Ted Cassidy, who played Lurch on the Addams Family, played basketball at what university?

25 Boxball? Naismith instructed Pop to find some boxes to hang in the gymnasium, but Pop could only find two peach baskets.

26 Dr. Luther Halsey Gulick, Jr., the director of the Springfield, Massachusetts YMCA.

27 University of Delaware

28 Centenary, with an enrollment under 1,000 students

29 The University of Pittsburgh

30 He made a three-point basket during a trial period being used by the Southern Conference

31 Eleven

32 The Big Seven. Duh...

33 The 1989 University of Kansas team. Kansas was put on probation for recruiting violations and one of the stipulations was that they were not allowed to participate in the NCAA tournament for one year.

34 California has 20 schools in NCAA Division I basketball. New York is second with 19.

35 The University of California-Los Angeles

36 Kareem Abdul-Jabbar formerly known as Lew Alcindor

37 Stetson University

3-PT **38** Tom Payne, a seven-foot All-American from Louisville, signed on June 9, 1969, with the University of Kentucky. Why was this important?

3-PT **39** How many games did Lew Alcindor's teams lose in his three seasons at UCLA?

3-PT **40** Former Supreme Court Justice Byron (Whizzer) White played in the NIT for what school?

3-PT **41** Otto Graham, member of the NFL's Hall of Fame, earned All-American status in 1944 as a basketball forward at what university?

3-PT **42** The Busch "bragging rights" trophy is awarded traditionally to the winner of what game?

3-PT **43** What player has performed for two different teams in the NCAA championship game?

3-PT **44** Nebraska head basketball coach Danny Nee was a high school teammate of what great New York prep star?

2-PT **45** Actor Tom Selleck was once a walk-on basketball player at what university?

3-PT **46** What former Division I head coach owns the original copy of Martin Luther King's "I have a dream" speech?

2-PT **47** At what college did Curt Gowdy excel in basketball?

3-PT **48** Lou Boudreau, better known as being a Hall of Fame baseball player, was a first team All-American forward and team captain at what university in 1938?

3-PT **49** What man, better known as the founder of the NFL, was a regular on the University of Illinois basketball team in 1917-18?

3-PT **50** Who is the first Heisman Trophy winner to play in the Final Four?

38 Tom Payne was the first African-American basketball player to sign at the University of Kentucky.

39 Two

40 Although known mainly for his football skills, Whizzer was also a mainstay on the Colorado Buffaloes basketball team.

41 Northwestern University

42 The Missouri-Illinois game

43 Bob Bender played in the 1976 championship game for Indiana and in the 1978 game for Duke.

44 Lew Alcindor, later known as Kareem Abdul-Jabbar

45 The University of Southern California

46 George Raveling now an analyst with CBS sports.

47 The University of Wyoming

48 The University of Illinois

49 George Halas

50 Terry Baker, of Oregon State, in 1963

3-PT **51** What is the first school to play for the national championship in both football and basketball in the same school year?

3-PT **52** What Grambling player scored more points in his career than Pete Maravich and grabbed more rebounds in his career than Robert Parish?

2-PT **53** What university did Dick Vitale attend?

2-PT **54** On March 29, 1945, the game between DePaul and Oklahoma A&M at Madison Square Garden was billed as the "Clash of Titans." Who were the titans?

3-PT **55** What University of Wyoming player from the 1945-1946 season is credited with creating the jumpshot?

3-PT **56** On April 25, 1950, Chuck Cooper became the first African-American player ever picked in the professional draft. For what school did Cooper play?

3-PT **57** Why was the NCAA championship almost postponed on March 30, 1981, at the Spectrum in Philadelphia, Pennsylvania?

2-PT **58** What two-time NCAA champion dropped its men's basketball program on July 29, 1982?

3-PT **59** On June 22, 1987, Baltimore's Dunbar High had 3 members of its 1982 team taken in the first round of the NBA draft. Name two of these players.

3-PT **60** What was part of the official flight kit of the space shuttle Discovery on March 13, 1989?

3-PT **61** Prior to committing to UCLA, Lew Alcindor had all but committed to what college, where he would have played for its legendary coach, Bob Cousy?

2-PT **62** What TV broadcaster announced all the Final Four games from 1965 to 1978?

51 Oklahoma played Kansas in the NCAA championship and Miami (Florida) in the Orange Bowl in 1988. They were denied a national championship both times.

52 Bob Hopkins, playing from 1953 to 1956 for NAIA school Grambling (now a Division I school)

53 Mr. Vitale graduated from Seton Hall in 1962.

54 George Mikan, of DePaul, clashed with Bob Kurland, of Oklahoma A&M, as A&M won 52-44.

55 Kenny Sailors

56 Duquesne

57 Because of an assassination attempt on President Ronald Reagan

58 The University of San Francisco. They brought the program back for the 1985-86 season.

59 Reggie Williams, of Georgetown, Tyrone Bogues, of Wake Forest, and the late Reggie Lewis, of Northeastern

60 An official Spalding Hall of Fame basketball

61 Boston College

62 Curt Gowdy

3-PT **63** What television program broadcast the NCAA Final Four on tape-delay from 1962 to 1965?

3-PT **64** Prior to the NBA players participation in 1992, who are the only two American players to compete on two Olympic teams?

3-PT **65** What is the only top-ranked team to decline a berth in the NCAA tournament?

2-PT **66** What is the first state to have more than six different schools reach the Final Four?

3-PT **67** Who was the first player to play for a NCAA champion and in a World Series?

3-PT **68** Who was the first player to lead a championship team in scoring in two Final Four games and pitch in the major leagues in the same season?

3-PT **69** Who was the first Final Four Most Outstanding Player to later have a brother inducted into the NFL Hall of Fame?

2-PT **70** Who was the first All-Tournament selection to finish his college playing career at another university?

3-PT **71** Who was the first leading scorer of a Final Four team to also play in a New Year's Day bowl game and win a silver medal in the Olympics as a high jumper?

2-PT **72** Who was the first seven-foot player to lead a Final Four in scoring and win a conference high jump title in the same year?

3-PT **73** Who was the first player to post the highest scoring game in an NCAA tournament the same year he played major league baseball?

3-PT **74** What major league baseball Hall of Fame inductee played one season of freshman basketball at the University of Cincinnati under coach Ed Jucker?

2-PT **75** What two professional sports did former University of Kansas center Wilt Chamberlain play?

63 ABC's Wide World of Sports

64 Bob Kurland, of Oklahoma A&M and Bill Houglin of Kansas. Both players remained eligible because of their amateur status.

65 Kentucky declined a bid in 1954.

66 Pennsylvania with Duquesne, La Salle, Pennsylvania, Penn State, St. Joseph's, Temple and Villanova.

67 Tim Stoddard played for North Carolina State in 1974 and pitched for the Baltimore Orioles in 1979.

68 Carl Bouldin, of Cincinnati

69 Alex Groza, of Kentucky, was named MOP in 1948 and 1949; his brother Lou is a member of the NFL Hall of Fame.

70 Vanderbilt guard Bill McCaffrey earned All-Tournament honors with Duke in 1991.

71 Dwight (Dike) Eddleman, of Illinois

72 Wilt Chamberlain, of Kansas

73 Dave DeBusschere, of Detroit

74 Sandy Koufax

75 Basketball and volleyball

3-PT **76** What former Seton Hall player became the first player in the NBA to shatter a backboard?

2-PT **77** In addition to basketball, Wilt Chamberlain lettered in what other sport at Kansas?

2-PT **78** What Creighton basketball standout went on to become one of the greatest pitchers in St. Louis Cardinal baseball history?

2-PT **79** What Minnesota player was drafted into the NFL, the NBA, and major league baseball?

2-PT **80** What Georgetown Hoya later became an NFL commissioner?

3-PT **81** What Tennessee All-American selection in 1967 became an NFL punter?

3-PT **82** What Dallas Cowboy has scored more points at Michigan State than Magic Johnson?

3-PT **83** What Stanford great starred with Betty Grable in the 1939 classic, "Campus Confessions?"

2-PT **84** What is responsible for the absence of fans from two games in the North Atlantic Conference Tournament in the 1988-89 season?

3-PT **85** What Hill Street Blues regular was on the 1967 and 1968 national champion UCLA Bruins?

3-PT **86** What future Baltimore Oriole scored 8 points for North Carolina State in their 1974 national championship game?

3-PT **87** What two schools have had two different players lead the nation in scoring in consecutive years?

3-PT **88** What great NFL quarterback was a consensus All-American in basketball at Northwestern in 1944?

3-PT **89** Rich Richman played for what school's football team in the Liberty Bowl and then on its basketball team a few hours later?

76 Chuck Connors, of the Boston Celtics, better known as the Rifleman

77 Track

78 Bob Gibson

79 Dave Winfield, who opted to play major league baseball.

80 Paul Tagliabue

81 Ron Widby

82 Pete Gent

83 Hank Luisetti

84 Measles

85 Michael Warren

86 Tim Stoddard

87 Furman and Loyola Marymount. For Furman, Frank Selvy ('54) and Darrall Floyd ('55). For Loyola Marymount, Hank Gathers ('89) and Bo Kimble ('90).

88 Otto Graham

89 Villanova, on December 15, 1962

3-PT **90** What is the only former NCAA champion that is no longer classified as a Division I college?

2-PT **91** What two teams from the same state played each other for the NCAA title in 1961 and 1962?

3-PT **92** Who was the second-leading scorer on Wake Forest's 1962 Final Four team? (He now works in broadcasting.)

2-PT **93** In 1959, Mississippi State finished their season at 24-1, won their conference title at 14-1, and were ranked No. 3 in the final AP poll. Why didn't they play in the NCAA tournament?

3-PT **94** What member of the Football Hall of Fame participated in the first public basketball game on March 11, 1892?

2-PT **95** In 1959, Pat Kennedy became the first what elected to the Basketball Hall of Fame?

3-PT **96** Who was the first individual enshrined into the Basketball Hall of Fame in two separate categories?

3-PT **97** What former major league pitcher was named to the Naismith Memorial Basketball Hall of Fame in 1982?

2-PT **98** Who was the first player or coach to be elected to both the football and basketball halls of fame?

3-PT **99** What Stanford Hall of Fame football player was also a star on the basketball team in the 1924-25 season?

2-PT **100** What team elected to cancel the remaining games on its schedule after a tragic plane accident in December 1977?

2-PT **101** What two teams played in the first college game to attract over 50,000 fans?

2-PT **102** In 1970, South Carolina finished at 25-3 and were undefeated in the ACC. Why did they not play in the NCAA tournament?

2-PT **103** What did Mike Pflugner of Butler do only 1:38 into a game against Illinois-Chicago on March 2, 1996?

90 City College of New York

91 Cincinnati and Ohio State

92 Billy Packer

93 They declined the offer to play. The State of Mississippi forbade the university from playing against desegregated teams.

94 Amos Alonzo Stagg

95 The first referee

96 On April 26, 1972, John Wooden was inducted as a coach, having already been inducted as a player in 1960.

97 Dave DeBusschere

98 Amos Alonzo Stagg

99 Ernie Nevers

100 The University of Evansville

101 Houston and UCLA, in the Houston Astrodome, on January 20, 1968

102 They lost in the ACC tournament when only the conference tournament champion advanced.

103 He picked up his fifth foul and was disqualified.

CHAPTER 5
PLACES

 1 In what city is the University of North Carolina located?

 2 The 1991 Final Four was held in what city?

 3 The University of Oregon plays basketball at McArthur Court. What is the nickname of McArthur Court?

 4 New Mexico State plays in what arena?

 5 In what arena does the University of Illinois play basketball?

 6 In what arena does Vanderbilt University play basketball?

 7 In what arena does Brigham Young University play its home games?

 8 In what arena does Ohio State University play its home games?

 9 In what town is Oregon State University located?

1 Chapel Hill, a small town located in the Piedmont of North Carolina.

2 In Indianapolis at the RCA Dome, located in the heart of downtown Indianapolis. Unlike most domed stadiums, the RCA Dome was built by the city as a much-needed expansion to the convention center, not as a stand-alone sporting venue.

3 The "Pit", built in 1926 and named for the university's first student-body president, McArthur Court is one of the oldest on-campus arenas.

4 The Pan-American Center, which received its name from Paul Rader, a former NMSU vice president who named it because of its position along Interstate 25, also known as the Pan American Highway.

5 In Assembly Hall, a multipurpose building built for concerts, convocations, theater, men's basketball and other sporting events; it has a 16,000 seat capacity and has a dome that spans 400 feet.

6 Memorial Gymnasium which was dedicated in 1952 as a memorial to all Vanderbilt men and women who served in World War II. Memorial Gymnasium also contains a wellness center for Vanderbilt employees, an auxiliary gym, and a six-lane swimming pool.

7 The Marriott Center, named for successful Utah businessman J. Willard Marriott, consistently ranks in the top ten in ticket sales nationally and is one of the largest on-campus facilities nation-wide.

8 St. John Arena, completed in November of 1956 at a cost of less than $4,000,000, the 13,276-seat structure is named for former OSU basketball coach and athletic director, L. W. St. John.

9 Nestled in the green, fertile Willamette Valley, Corvallis enjoys mild temperatures and easy access to the Pacific Ocean, the Cascade Mountains, the high desert of Eastern Oregon and the big city amenities of Portland and Eugene.

10 In what arena does the University of Arizona play its home games?

 11 In what arena does UCLA play its home games?

 12 What is the home court of Duke University?

 13 What is the home arena of the University of North Carolina?

 14 What state has produced more NCAA Division I basketball champions than any other?

 15 Name the home arena for the University of Minnesota.

 16 What is the name of the home arena for Indiana University?

 17 What is the home court for the University of Iowa?

 18 Where did St. Joseph's unforgettable 1981 NCAA tournament upset of number one DePaul take place?

 19 Where is St. Joseph's University located?

 20 Kansas State's Bramlage Coliseum opened Nov. 26, 1988. In what fieldhouse did Kansas State play their games before 1988?

10 McKale Memorial Center, the home of Wildcat basketball, opened in February of 1973 with a seating capacity of 13,658 (14, 459 current). The facility is named in memory of the late J.F. "Pop" McKale, who was UA athletic director and coach from 1914 to 1957.

11 Pauley Pavilion, which was named for Edwin W. Pauley, who contributed $1 million to its construction. The pavilion was first used in 1966 and seats 12,500. In 1984, it was the site of the gymnastics competition during the summer Olympic games.

12 Cameron Indoor Stadium which opened on January 6, 1940.

13 The on campus arena is called the Dean E. Smith Center and opened on January 18, 1986. The No. 1-ranked Tar Heels opened the 21,572-seat arena by beating No. 3 Duke, 95-92.

14 California, with 15 banners.

15 Williams Arena was completed in 1928, then it was known as Minnesota Field House. It cost $650,000 and seated 14,100. The building was remodeled in 1950 and renamed in honor of Dr. Henry L. Williams, U of M football coach from 1900 to 1921.

16 Home of basketball's "Hurryin' Hoosiers," Assembly Hall is a 17,500-seat multipurpose building that also hosts women's home basketball games, the Little 500 Tricycle Race, and occasional rock concerts.

17 Carver-Hawkeye Arena, opened in January of 1983, is named for the late Roy Carver a long-time supporter of the University.

18 Dayton, Ohio

19 Philadelphia, Pennsylvania

20 In Ahearn Fieldhouse. The building was the product of a 10-year drive by several people, most notably athletic director Mike Ahearn and head basketball coach Jack Gardner. The two-million dollar structure opened on Dec. 9, 1950, when K-State defeated Utah.

21 Brewer Field House was the home of the Missouri Tigers from 1930 to 1972. What arena became their home arena in 1973?

 22 Temple University is located in what city?

 23 What fieldhouse does the University of Kansas call home?

 24 Name the home arena for the Georgetown Hoyas.

 25 What state does East Carolina State University call home?

 26 In what state does Western Carolina play its home basketball games?

 27 Iona College is located in what city?

 28 What town is the final resting place of basketball legends James Naismith and Dr. Forrest Allen?

 29 What three states do not have representatives in NCAA Division I basketball?

 30 Jackson State University is located in what state?

 31 In what city is Northeastern University located?

 32 What university is located in Starkville, Mississippi?

 33 In what state is Morgan State?

21   Hearnes Center. The complex, officially the Warren E. Hearnes Multipurpose Building, was dedicated by Governor Hearnes on Aug. 4, 1972. The Tigers followed with an 87-75 triumph over Ohio University on Nov. 25, 1972.

22   Philadelphia, Pennsylvania

23   In Allen Fieldhouse where a crowd of 17,228 Jayhawks fans cheered as KU defeated the Kansas State Wildcats 77-66 in the first game at the arena in 1955. Five million fans later, the fieldhouse remains one of the best atmospheres for college basketball.

24   Capitol Centre

25   North Carolina

26   North Carolina

27   In New Rochelle, New York

28   Lawrence, Kansas. The final resting places of these basketball legends are only blocks apart.

29   Only Alaska, North Dakota, and South Dakota do not have representatives in Division I basketball.

30   Mississippi (Jackson, Mississippi).

31   Boston, also known as "Beantown," the "Hub," and the "Athens of America".

32   Mississippi State University.

33   Maryland (Baltimore)

3-PT **34** Who is LSU's home arena named after?

3-PT **35** Stetson University is located in what state?

2-PT **36** In what state is Pepperdine University located?

2-PT **37** On what campus was the first NCAA post-season championship tournament held?

2-PT **38** The U.S. Naval Academy is located in what city?

2-PT **39** In what city did Larry Bird and Magic Johnson battle it out as Indiana State and Michigan State played for the NCAA title in 1979?

2-PT **40** Where is Brown University located?

3-PT **41** In what city is Siena College located?

2-PT **42** Old Dominion University is located in what state?

2-PT **43** In what state would you find Bowling Green University?

3-PT **44** In what state is Radford University located?

3-PT **45** Monmouth College is located where?

3-PT **46** Fairfield University is located in what state?

34 Pete Maravich

35 Florida

36 Located in Malibu, California, Pepperdine University is an independent, Christian University, enrolling about 6,500 students in four colleges and schools.

37 Northwestern University

38 In Annapolis, Maryland, the state capital and also known as the "sailboat capital of the world". Annapolis is the home of the United States Naval Academy, and Saint John's College and is located at the mouth of the Severn River on the Chesapeake Bay.

39 In Salt Lake City, Utah

40 Providence, Rhode Island

41 Loudonville, New York

42 Virginia

43 Ohio

44 Virginia (Radford)

45 In West Long Branch, New Jersey

46 Connecticut

CHAPTER 6
NICKNAMES

 1 How many Division I schools are nicknamed the Bulldogs? Is it 4, 8, 12, or 16?

 2 How many Division I schools are nicknamed the Tigers? Is it 9, 11, or 13?

 3 How many Division I schools are nicknamed the Wildcats?

 4 What was Oscar Robertson's nickname?

 5 What was the nickname of Oklahoma A&M's seven-foot tall Bob Kurland?

 6 What was Nate Archibald's nickname?

 7 What was the nickname of Jack Givens, the MOP on Kentucky's 1978 NCAA title team?

 8 What is Magic Johnson's given first name?

 9 What is the nickname of the University of Arizona?

 10 What is the nickname of Wake Forest University?

 11 Two Division I schools are nicknamed the Broncs. Name one of them.

 12 Two Division I schools are nicknamed the Bruins. Name one of them.

 13 Three Division I schools are nicknamed the Lions. Name one of them.

1 Twelve

2 Eleven

3 Nine

4 The Big O

5 Foothills

6 Tiny

7 "Goose"

8 Earvin

9 In 1914 a student correspondent for the Los Angeles Times, covering the Arizona-Occidental football game on the Occidental campus, wrote... "The Arizona men showed the fight of wildcats." After reading the story back in Tucson, a resolution was drawn up and passed that Arizona athletic teams would be called the Wildcats.

10 The Demon Deacons. The teams were once known as the Baptists and the Old Gold and Black. In 1924 the editor of the school paper first called the team the Demon Deacons after a win over Trinity (now Duke).

11 Texas-Pan American and Rider College

12 Brown and UCLA

13 Columbia, Loyola Marymount, and Southeastern Louisiana

14 What nickname is used by more Division I basketball programs than any other?

 15 What school is nicknamed the Gentlemen, or the Gents?

 16 What team plays its home games in an arena nicknamed "The Deaf Dome"?

 17 Name two schools that are nicknamed the Aggies.

 18 Who was the "Iron Duke?"

 19 What is named "Handsome Dan" and patrols the baseline at Yale basketball games?

 20 What is the nickname of Howard University?

 21 What is Creighton's team nickname?

 22 What is the nickname of North Carolina State University?

 23 What is the nickname of Michigan State University?

 24 Two Division I schools are nicknamed the Bisons. Name one of them.

 25 Two Division I schools are nicknamed the Braves. Name one of them.

 26 Two Division I schools are nicknamed the Dukes. Name one of them.

 27 Two Division I schools are nicknamed the Hornets. Name one of them.

14 Bulldogs, which is the nickname of twelve schools

15 Centenary College

16 Louisiana State University

17 Texas A&M, Utah State, North Carolina A&T State, and New Mexico State

18 Henry Iba, famed head basketball coach at Oklahoma State.

19 A bulldog. The first live Yale bulldog, Handsome Dan, was introduced in 1889.

20 The Bison. The name Bison was a nickname Indians bequeathed to black regiments during the Indian Wars because these soldiers represented the best in fighting spirit.

21 The Bluejays. Prior to 1924, the Creighton teams were known as the Hilltoppers. Billy Bluejay, as he is known affectionately throughout the university campus, is the official symbol of the men's teams.

22 The Wolfpack. In the early days, they called State's varisty teams the Farmers & Mechanics, the Aggies, or the Techs, but most often they called them the Red Terrors.

23 The Spartans. Standing at the entrance way of Michigan State's athletic facilities is "The Spartan" a huge statue which symbolizes the universities athletic teams.

24 Bucknell and Howard

25 Alcorn State and Bradley

26 Duquesne and James Madison

27 California State-Sacramento and Delaware State

28 Two Division I schools are nicknamed the Lumberjacks. Name one of them.

29 Two Division I schools are nicknamed the Titans. Name one of them.

30 Three Division I schools are nicknamed the Mountaineers. Name one of them.

31 What is Bobby Knight's nickname?

32 Two Division I schools are nicknamed the Jaguars. Name one of them.

33 Nine Division I schools are nicknamed the Wildcats. Name four of them.

34 Name three of the players known as the "Fab Five" at Michigan.

35 What is the nickname of Vanderbilt University?

36 What is the nickname of Duke University?

37 What player nicknamed "Sleepy" played guard for Georgetown in 1982?

38 What is the nickname of the University of Washington?

39 What is the nickname of the University of North Carolina?

40 What is the nickname of Lehigh University?

28 Northern Arizona and Stephen F. Austin

29 California State University at Fullerton and University of Detroit Mercy

30 Appalachian State, Mount St. Mary's College, and West Virginia

31 The General

32 South Alabama and Southern University

33 Arizona, Bethune-Cookman College, Davidson, Kansas State, Kentucky, New Hampshire, Northwestern, Villanova, and Weber State

34 Chris Webber, Jalen Rose, Jimmy King, Ray Jackson, and Juwan Howard

35 The Commodores. The school was founded by Commodore Cornelius Vanderbilt. The name Commodores was first applied to Vanderbilt teams by William E. Beard when he was a member of a local newspaper editorial staff in 1897.

36 The Blue Devils. Through the persistence of the student newspaper editors in 1922-23, Duke University is called the Blue Devils. Prior to that, the teams were called the Methodists and Blue and White.

37 Eric Floyd

38 The Huskies. The name came about in 1921 from a committee of team captains, coaches and faculty members. The group narrowed a long list of suggestions to the Malamutes and Huskies, before adopting Huskies. Prior to 1921, the teams were known as the Sundodgers.

39 The Tar Heels. Teams at UNC are known as the Tar Heels because North Carolina is the "Tar Heel State." The nickname is said to have been applied to the area's residents during the Revolutionary War.

40 The Engineers. The nickname is symbolic of the school's engineering excellence.

41 What is the nickname for Indiana University?

 42 Name two schools that are nicknamed the Cardinals.

 43 Two Division I schools are nicknamed the Colonels. Name one of them.

 44 Two Division I schools are nicknamed the Gaels. Name one of them.

 45 Three Division I schools are nicknamed the Golden Eagles. Name one of them.

 46 Who was the "Big E?"

 47 What guard, whose nickname was "the surgeon," was the first Kansas player to participate in four NCAA tournaments?

 48 What player nicknamed Butch led Marquette to the NCAA Final Four in 1977?

 49 What is Marshall's team nickname?

 50 What two schools are nicknamed the 49ers?

 51 Name five Division I schools nicknamed the Bulldogs.

 52 What is the nickname of the University of Illinois?

 53 What is the nickname of the Navy basketball team?

41 The Hoosiers. There are at least eight versions on the origin of the name. Probably the most valid is that a canal builder along the Ohio named Sam Hoosier hired a lot of Indiana workers. When they brawled with Kentucky workers the rallying cry was, "Hoosier, Hoosier."

42 Louisville, Lamar, and Ball State

43 Eastern Kentucky and Nicholls State

44 Iona College and St. Mary's College

45 Northeastern Illinois, Southern Mississippi, and Tennessee Tech

46 Elvin Hayes, who gained fame for head coach Guy Lewis at the University of Houston.

47 Mark Turgeon, who was the first recruit signed by Larry Brown at Kansas.

48 Alfred Lee

49 The Thundering Herd. A former sports editor and columnist of the *Huntington Herald-Dispatch* took the name from the title of one of Zane Grey's Old West novels.

50 Long Beach State and the University of North Carolina-Charlotte

51 Butler, The Citadel, Drake, Fresno State, Georgia, Gonzaga, Louisiana Tech , Mississippi State, North Carolina-Asheville, Samford, South Carolina State, and Yale

52 The Fighting Illini. Chief Illiniwek is one of the most colorful traditions in college athletics. His dramatic war dance is a highlight of football and basketball games.

53 The Midshipmen. Although two cats, a dog and a carrier pigeon have enjoyed brief reigns as the Navy mascot, goats have served without interruption since 1904.

54 Two Division I schools are nicknamed the Terriers. Name one of them.

 55 What was the nickname of the 1940 national championship Indiana team?

 56 What is Furman's team nickname?

 57 What are Georgia Tech's two acceptable team nicknames?

 58 What team was known as the "Fiddlers Five?"

 59 Two Division I schools are nicknamed the Knights. Name one of them.

 60 Two Division I schools are nicknamed the Pirates. Name one of them.

 61 Four Division I schools are nicknamed the Panthers. Name one of them.

 62 Name five Division I schools that are nicknamed the Tigers.

 63 What city is known officially as "Basketball City, USA?"

 64 What player nicknamed "The Fly" led Austin Peay to two NCAA tournament appearances?

 65 What North Carolina State player was nicknamed "Skywalker"?

 66 What is the nickname of the University of Southern California?

67 What is the nickname of Penn State University?

54 Boston University and St. Francis College

55 The Hurryin' Hoosiers

56 The Paladins. Furman athletic teams were known by different names until the 1961 school year. The baseball team was the Hornets, the football team the Hurricanes and the basketball team the Paladins.

57 The Ramblin' Wreck and the Yellowjackets. The name "Ramblin'Wreck" grew out of an old drinking ballad called "The Sons of Gamboliers."

58 The 1958 Kentucky Wildcats, coached by Adolph Rupp. The starting lineup included Vern Hatton, Adrian Smith, Johnny Cox, John Crigler and Ed Beck.

59 Central Florida and Fairleigh Dickinson

60 East Carolina and Seton Hall

61 Eastern Illinois, Northern Iowa, Pittsburgh, and Prairie View A&M

62 Auburn, Clemson, Grambling St., Jackson St., Louisiana St., Memphis, Missouri, Pacific, Princeton, Tennessee St., Texas Southern, and Towson St.

63 Springfield, Massachusetts - home of the basketball hall of fame.

64 James Williams led the Governors and head coach Lake Kelley to the tournament in 1972-73 and 1973-74.

65 David Thompson

66 The Trojans. When the USC band plays "Conquest" during a football game, everyone in the Los Angeles Coliseum knows what is going to happen. Traveller III, USC's mascot, explodes out of the tunnel and around the field.

67 The Nittany Lions. Because Penn State is located in the Nittany Valley at the foot of Mount Nittany, the team was called the Nittany Lions. The lion was chosen by the student body in 1906. The lion is said to have roamed the central Pennsylvania mountains.

CHAPTER 7
TOURNEYS

 1 What Indiana Hoosier guard scored 19 of his 23 points in the second half of the 1981 NCAA championship game against North Carolina?

 2 When was the consolation game added to the finals of the NCAA Basketball Tournament?

 3 Who led UNLV to the NCAA championship in 1990 by scoring 29 points in the championship game?

 4 What university won the first NCAA basketball championship?

 5 What two Big Eight schools played for the 1988 NCAA championship?

 6 What team won back-to-back NCAA championships in 1961 and 1962? (Hint: They defeated Ohio State in both national championship games).

 7 How many overtime periods were played in the 1957 NCAA championship game between North Carolina and Kansas?

 8 What was the only school to make four appearances during the 1980s in the NCAA Final Four?

 9 Who did the Marquette Warriors beat to win the NCAA championship in 1977?

 10 What Big East opponent upset the Georgetown Hoyas for the NCAA championship in 1985?

 11 What college team made it to the NCAA championship game in 1983 and 1984 but did not win?

 12 Which is older, the National Invitational Tournament (NIT) or the NCAA championship?

1 Sophomore point guard Isiah Thomas, who also contributed five assists and four steals in leading the Hoosiers to a 63-50 victory over North Carolina.

2 It came in 1946 as Ohio State defeated California, 63-45. In the national championship game that season, Oklahoma A&M defeated North Carolina, 43-40.

3 Anderson Hunt led UNLV to a 103-73 victory over Duke and was named Most Outstanding Player of the tournament.

4 Oregon and coach Howard "Hobby" Hobson defeated Ohio State in 1939. It was an eight-team tournament held in Evanston, Illinois. The tournament attracted a combined 15,025 fans.

5 Kansas and Oklahoma played in the 50th NCAA Final Four. The Jayhawks, under head coach Larry Brown and standout player Danny Manning, defeated the Sooners, 83-79.

6 Ed Jucker's Cincinnati Bearcats defeated Ohio State 70-65 in 1961 and again the following season, 71-59.

7 North Carolina and its standout Lennie Rosenbluth prevailed in the third overtime over Wilt Chamberlain and the Kansas Jayhawks, 54-53. The game was played in Kansas City, Missouri.

8 The University of Louisville, which won the national championship with a 72-69 win over Duke in the 1986 Final Four.

9 Coach Al McGuire and his Marquette Warriors defeated Dean Smith and the North Carolina Tar Heels, 67-59.

10 In the first year that the tournament was expanded to 64 teams, Villanova - connecting on 22 of 28 field goal attempts - upset John Thompson and the Hoyas, 66-64.

11 The University of Houston. North Carolina State upset Coach Guy Lewis and the Cougars, 54-52, in 1983. Georgetown won the title from Houston in 1984 with a 84-75 victory.

12 The NIT is a year older, starting during the 1937-38 season.

13 What was the first New England-based team to win the NCAA championship?

 14 Who was the first Southeast Conference team to win the NIT?

 15 In 1985, three Big East teams were in the Final Four. Name the only non-Big East team in the field.

 16 Who were the three Big East teams that participated in the 1985 Final Four?

 17 UCLA won the NCAA championship 10 times in 12 years, from 1964 to 1975. Who were the two other teams to win NCAA championships during that period?

 18 Five UCLA players have been named the Most Outstanding Player in the NCAA Final Four. Name the three other than Bill Walton and Lew Alcindor.

 19 The gate gross for five nights of basketball at the 1942 NCAA tournament was: (a) $50,500, (b) $75,500, or (c) $23,500?

 20 In 1976, Indiana entered the NCAA tournament undefeated at 27-0. What other team entered the same tournament undefeated with a 28-0 record?

 21 Name four of the starting five for North Carolina's 1982 national championship team.

 22 Since 1956, NCAA Final Four competitors came from four different regions. Which region has produced the most national champions?

 23 Which arena has hosted the most NCAA tournament games?

 24 Which state has hosted the most national championship games?

25 What is the only school to advance to the Final Four in its only appearance in the NCAA tournament?

13 Holy Cross, coached by Doggie Julian, defeated Oklahoma, 58-47, to win the 1947 NCAA title.

14 Vanderbilt, in 1990, was the first SEC team to win the NIT.

15 Memphis State

16 Villanova, Georgetown, and St. John's

17 Texas Western (Texas-El Paso) in 1966 and North Carolina State in 1974.

18 Walt Hazzard, Sidney Wicks, and Richard Washington

19 (c) $23,500: Stanford University's share of the '42 pot after expenses and division among participating teams was $93.75

20 Rutgers

21 Matt Doherty, James Worthy, Sam Perkins, Jimmy Black, and Michael Jordan

22 The Far West, or West, with 16

23 Municipal Auditorium in Kansas City, Missouri, was the site for 83 games from 1940 to 1964.

24 Missouri with 12

25 Indiana State, led by the legendary Larry Bird, made it all the way to the championship game against Michigan State in 1979. It was their first and only trip to the NCAA tournament.

Walt Hazzard

26 Only one player has been named the Most Outstanding Player of the Final Four three times. Who is he?

 27 What two teams from the Big Ten played in the national championship game in 1976?

28 The winner of the first Army-Navy basketball game every year wins what?

29 What three arenas have hosted considerably more national championships than any others?

 30 Name the one team from the District of Columbia that has won the national championship.

31 Name the school that has made five Final Four appearances without winning a title.

 32 In what year was the NCAA championship game televised nationally for the first time? Was it 1947, 1954, 1959, or 1963?

33 What two teams from the same conference met in 1985 for the NCAA championship?

34 Two freshmen have been named the Most Outstanding Player in the Final Four. One was Arnie Ferrin in 1944 from Utah. Who was the other?

35 What is the record for overtimes in a national championship game?

36 The 1982 NCAA All-Tournament Team brought together what five players who would become great pros? (Hint: Three from North Carolina, two from Georgetown.)

 37 Who were the two undefeated teams entering the NCAA tournament in 1971?

 38 Who won the first National Invitational Tournament?

26 Lew Alcindor, of UCLA, in 1967, 1968, and 1969

27 Coach Bob Knight's Indiana Hoosiers defeated conference rival Michigan, 86-68, to claim the national championship.

28 The Alumni Trophy

29 Municipal Auditorium, in Kansas City; Madison Square Garden, in New York City; and Freedom Hall, in Louisville

30 Georgetown

31 The Houston Cougars

32 It happened in 1954 when La Salle, led by All-American Tom Gola, defeated Bradley, 92-76 in Kansas City, Missouri

33 Georgetown and Villanova

34 Pervis Ellison of Louisville led his team to the national championship against heavily favored Duke in 1986.

35 North Carolina beat Kansas and its star center - Wilt Chamberlain - 54-53 after three overtimes in 1957.

36 James Worthy, Michael Jordan, Sam Perkins, Patrick Ewing, and Eric Floyd

37 Marquette and Pennsylvania

38 Temple beat Colorado 60-36 in 1938

39 On April 1, 1943, the NIT and NCAA champions played each other in a benefit game. What was that game called?

 40 Who is the only team to win back-to-back NIT championships?

 41 In 1944, which team lost in the first round of the NIT but then went on to win the NCAA championship?

 42 Which stadium was the first in NCAA history to hold over 20,000 spectators?

 43 What building held both the NIT and NCAA tournament in 1950?

 44 Who was the first NCAA champion to finish the season undefeated?

 45 What Temple player was the first player not to participate in the NCAA championship game and still be named the tournament MVP?

 46 Who was the Most Outstanding Player of the 1993 NCAA tournament?

 47 In what year was the Final Four first held in a domed stadium? Was it 1971, 1973, or 1983?

 48 Who started at center for Marquette in their 1977 NCAA championship win over North Carolina?

 49 The first time that four teams gathered at the same site for the NCAA tournament semifinals and final was in 1946. Where were those games played?

 50 What is the largest margin of victory in an NCAA championship final? Hint: It's an even number.

 51 Who was the last team to hold sole possession of third place in the NCAA tournament?

 52 What player tipped in the winning basket in overtime in the 1963 championship game to give Loyola a 60-58 win over two-time defending champion Cincinnati?

39 The Red Cross Benefit Game, in which NCAA champion
Wyoming beat NIT champion St. John's.

40 St. John's in 1943 and 1944

41 Utah

42 Chicago Stadium on March 23, 1946, took in 22,828 people
for a game in which Ohio State defeated Northwestern.

43 Madison Square Garden in New York City.

44 San Francisco, in 1956. The Dons were led by All-American
center Bill Russell, who scored 26 points in their 83-71
victory over Iowa in the national championship game.

45 Hal Lear, in 1956. Lear scored 160 points in the tournament
- averaging 32 per game - including 48 versus SMU.

46 Donald Williams, of North Carolina

47 1971 in the Astrodome as UCLA defeated Villanova, 68-62.

48 Jerome Whitehead

49 Madison Square Garden which hosted Ohio State, North
Carolina, California and eventual national champion
Oklahoma A&M.

50 UNLV beat Duke by thirty, 103-73, in 1990.

51 Virginia in 1981 (the NCAA consolation game was
discontinued beginning with the 1982 Final Four)

52 Vic Rouse tipped in a miss by Les Hunter.

53 In what year was the Final Four championship game first played at night?

 54 What player never led his team in scoring average in any of his three seasons and yet was Most Outstanding Player of the Final Four?

 55 Who is the leading scorer and rebounder among the seventy-nine people that have played and coached in the NCAA tournament?

 56 Who was the first player in NCAA tournament history to score more than 40 points and have more than 25 rebounds in the same game?

 57 In what year did two undefeated teams first reach the Final Four?

 58 How many NCAA tournaments netted a financial loss?

 59 Who was the Most Outstanding Player of the NCAA tournament in 1983, the year North Carolina State won the tournament? (Hint: He played for the University of Houston).

 60 Prior to the NCAA tournament, who decided who the number one team in the nation was?

 61 What does NIT stand for ?

 62 In a 64-team NCAA tournament, how many games must a team win to become the national champion?

 63 How many teams were included in each NCAA tournament from 1939 through 1950?

 64 What team won the NCAA title in 1976 and finished the year undefeated at 32-0?

 65 What school is credited with being the first collegiate "national champion"?

53 1970

54 Hakeem Olajuwon, of Houston

55 Jeff Mullins, who coached the University of North Carolina-Charlotte and played for Duke.

56 Elvin Hayes, of Houston, scored 49 points and had 27 rebounds against Loyola of Chicago in 1968.

57 1976 - Indiana and Rutgers

58 Only one and it was the first tournament in 1939 which lost $2,531.

59 Hakeem Olajuwon

60 The Helms Athletic Foundation

61 National Invitational Tournament

62 Six

63 Eight

64 Indiana

65 Columbia, by defeating Minnesota 27-15 and Wisconsin 21-15 in March, 1905

3-PT **66** How many NCAA national championship games have been decided in overtime?

2-PT **67** What two Big Ten teams played each other in the 1989 NCAA national semi-final?

3-PT **68** What four teams played in the 1989 Final Four?

3-PT **69** What two Big East Conference schools played each other in the 1987 NCAA national semi-final?

3-PT **70** What four teams played in the 1986 Final Four in Dallas?

3-PT **71** What four teams participated in the 1983 Final Four in Albuquerque?

3-PT **72** Who did UCLA play in the 1970 NCAA Championship game? (Note: Lew Alcindor had graduated from UCLA the previous year).

3-PT **73** What two teams entered the 1968 NCAA tournament with undefeated records?

2-PT **74** How many NCAA national champions have vacated the championship?

2-PT **75** How many NCAA runner-up teams have vacated their NCAA tournament games?

3-PT **76** Who set a NCAA tournament record by scoring 177 points in 1965?

2-PT **77** Who broke Bill Bradley's NCAA tournament scoring record in 1989?

2-PT **78** What was the first year Mississippi State participated in the NCAA tournament?

2-PT **79** What two former Big Eight schools have won NCAA national championships?

2-PT **80** Who was the first player to score 30 or more points in a NCAA championship game?

66 Six (1944, 1957, 1961, 1963, 1989, and 1997)

67 Michigan edged Illinois, 83-81, and went on to defeat Seton Hall, 80-79, in overtime to win the national championship.

68 Michigan, Illinois, Duke and Seton Hall

69 Syracuse defeated Providence, 77-63.

70 Louisiana State, Louisville, Duke, and Kansas. Lousiville defeated Duke to win the national championship.

71 Houston, Louisville, North Carolina State, and Georgia

72 The Bruins with new center Steve Patterson defeated Jacksonville - which featured 7-2 Artis Gilmore - in the national championship game, 80-69.

73 Houston and St. Bonaventure

74 None

75 Two. Villanova in 1971 and UCLA in 1980

76 Bill Bradley, of Princeton

77 Glen Rice, of Michigan, scored 184 points in the1989 tournament. Rice scored 31 points in the championship game to lead Michigan to a 80-79 win over Seton Hall.

78 1963. Prior to that time, the State of Mississippi forbade the university from playing against desegregated teams.

79 Kansas and Oklahoma State (formerly Oklahoma A & M)

80 Clyde Lovellette, of Kansas, scored 33 in the 1952 final.

CHAPTER 8
RECORDS

 1 What college All-American at Purdue once made 138 consecutive free throws in competition?

 2 How long was the UCLA winning streak the Houston Cougars snapped in 1968?

 3 What center broke Minnesota's individual scoring record with the most points in a career in 1978?

 4 Who set Kentucky's single-game scoring record against Ole Miss in 1970?

 5 As of 1997, what player held every Maryland rebounding record?

 6 Who holds the career record for rebounds at the University of San Francisco?

 7 What was it Todd Leslie made fifteen consecutive of to set an NCAA record over the course of four games during the 1990-91 season?

 8 Eric Crake, a 5-foot 10-inch guard for Georgia Tech, holds a record of 27 of what in a game?

 9 On December 21, 1989, Dave Jamerson of Ohio made 14 of what ?

 10 Ed Tooley, of Brown, attempted 36 of what in a game against Amherst on December 4, 1954?

 11 David Robinson of Navy and Shawn Bradley of Brigham Young have both done what 14 times in one game?

 12 Cincinnati and Bradley played the longest basketball game recorded on December 21, 1981. Was it five overtimes, seven overtimes or nine overtimes?

1 John Wooden

2 47 games

3 Mychal Thompson

4 Dan Issel, with 53 points

5 Len Elmore. Len graduated from law school and has gone on to become an outstanding announcer and color man for college basketball.

6 Bill Russell, with 1,606

7 Three-pointers

8 Rebounds

9 Three-pointers

10 Free throws

11 Blocked a shot

12 Seven overtime periods

Dan Issel

13 In 1992, what player shattered Bob Kurland's scoring record at Oklahoma State?

14 What Furman players were the leading scorers in the country in 1953, 1954, 1955 and 1956?

15 Chris Corchiani became the all-time NCAA assist leader in 1981, a record that has since been broken. At what school did he play?

16 In 1953, Bill Chambers, of William and Mary, had 51 of these in a game against Virginia. What were they?

17 Pete Maravich averaged more than 40 points a game for a season. Only two other players have done it. Name one of them.

18 Bruce Morris made an 89-foot, 10-inch shot that gave him the world record for the longest collegiate shot. At what university did Bruce Morris play?

19 In 1981, what Oregon State player shot 74.6 percent from the field, an all-time NCAA single season record?

20 On January 31, 1989, what two teams set these scoring records: 331 points by two teams, 150 points in a losing effort, 170 points by two teams in one half?

21 What player dished out his 1,039th assist on March 1, 1993, to break the all-time NCAA assist record?

22 What 6-foot 10-inch Kansas player set a NCAA record for most games (132) scoring in double digits during his career?

23 What 6-foot 2-inch Providence guard set the NCAA career record for most steals with 376 from 1988-91?

24 What 6-foot 5-inch All-American North Carolina player set a NCAA semifinal game record with 42 field goal attempts in 1957?

13 Byron Houston, with 2,379 points

14 Frank Selvy in 1953 and 1954, Darrel Floyd in 1955 and 1956

15 North Carolina State

16 Rebounds

17 Frank Selvy, of Furman, averaged 41.7 in 1954, and Johnny Neumann, of Mississippi, averaged 40.1 in 1971.

18 Marshall

19 Steve Johnson

20 Loyola Marymount and American International

21 Bobby Hurley, of Duke

22 Danny Manning

23 Eric Murdock

24 Len Rosenbluth, versus Michigan State

Bobby Hurley

25 What 6-foot Southern Illinois guard led the nation in free throw percentage in 1971 and 1972 and held the NCAA career record for highest free throw percentage at a 90.9 mark?

 26 What player set the career assists record at Virginia and later became the school's head coach?

 27 What player set a single-game rebounding record for Texas Western by pulling down 36 boards against Western New Mexico in 1964?

 28 Who holds the career record for blocked shots at Clemson? (Clue: It was like trying to shoot over one)

 29 On January 10, 1976, St. Joseph's of Pennsylvania had a record number of players disqualified due to fouls. Did they lose 8, 9, or 10 players?

 30 Through the 1991 season, what Loyola Marymount guard held the NCAA career record for most three-point field goals made and attempted?

 31 Since 1948, who are the only two players to lead the nation in scoring and rebounding in the same season?

 32 Who set a NCAA record by hitting 95.4 percent of his free throw attempts in 1985?

 33 What player, though only 6 feet 5 inches tall, set a NCAA record by averaging 25.6 rebounds per game in 1955?

 34 What Ohio University player set a NCAA record by hitting 14 three-point field goals in 1989 versus Charleston?

 35 Who set a NCAA Final Four single-game record for most blocked shots with six against Duke in 1988?

 36 Who set a NCAA tournament single-game record for assists, with 18 against Indiana, in 1987?

 37 Who set Louisville's single-game scoring record in 1967 against Georgetown?

25 Greg Starrick

26 Jeff Jones

27 Jim Barnes

28 Tree Rollins

29 They lost eight players.

30 Jeff Fryer

31 Xavier McDaniel, of Wichita State, and Hank Gathers, of Loyola Marymount

32 Craig Collins, of Penn State

33 Charlie Slack, of Marshall. He also led the nation in rebounding percentage in 1956, pulling down 23.6 per game.

34 Dave Jamerson

35 Danny Manning, of Kansas

36 Mark Wade, Of Nevada-Las Vegas

37 Wes Unseld, with 45 points

38 Who holds Michigan State's single-game assists record?

 39 Who set Michigan's single-game scoring record against Northwestern in 1966?

 40 Who set UNLV's single-game scoring record against Portland in 1967?

 41 Who set Kansas's single-game scoring record in 1956 against Northwestern in his first varsity game?

 42 Who set UCLA's single-game scoring record against Washington State in 1967?

 43 Who set Arizona's single-game scoring record against Cal State-LA in 1960?

 44 What Virginia Tech player set a NCAA record when he made at least one three-point field goal in 73 consecutive games?

 45 Who set Notre Dame's single-game scoring record against West Virginia in 1970?

 46 Who set Indiana's single-game scoring record against Minnesota in 1962 and matched this feat the next year against Michigan State?

 47 Who set St. John's single-game scoring record against St. Peter's in 1950?

 48 Who set Houston's single-game scoring record against Valparaiso in 1968?

 49 Who set Georgia Tech's single-game scoring record against Loyola Marymount in 1990?

 50 Who set Syracuse's single-game scoring record against Lafayette in 1971?

 51 Who set Georgetown's single-game scoring record against Fairleigh Dickinson in 1965?

52 Who set Oklahoma State's single-game scoring record against St. Louis in 1946?

38 Earvin "Magic" Johnson dished out 14 assists in three different games

39 Cazzie Russell, with 48 points

40 Elburt Miller, with 55 points

41 Wilt Chamberlain, with 52 points

42 Lew Alcindor, with 61 points

43 Ernie McCray, with 46 points

44 Wally Lancaster

45 Austin Carr, with 61 points

46 Jimmy Rayl, who scored 56 points in both games

47 Bob Zawoluk, with 65 points

48 Elvin Hayes, with 62 points

49 Kenny Anderson, with 50 points

50 Bill Smith, with 47 points

51 Jim Barry, with 46 points

52 Bob Kurland, with 58 points

Wilt Chamberlain

53 Who set Duke's single-game scoring record against Miami in 1988?

 54 Who set Ohio State's single-game scoring record against Illinois in 1964?

 55 Who set Cincinnati's single-game scoring record against North Texas State during the 1958-59 season?

 56 Who set Missouri's single-game scoring record against Nebraska in 1961?

 57 What team led the nation in rebound margin, with +11.1, in 1992-1993, for the third time in 7 years?

 58 Name in order the three NCAA Division I basketball all-time leaders in total victories.

 59 What school led the nation in scoring in the 1961-62 season at 91.8 points per game and in its 1962-63 national championship season at 90.2 points per game?

 60 What Oklahoma university led the nation in scoring in the 1983-84 season with a 90.8 scoring average?

 61 Who holds, at 60 games, the second-longest winning streak in NCAA history?

 62 What school was the first to win 1,000 basketball games?

 63 UCLA's 88-game winning streak ended on whose home floor?

 64 What Big Ten school led the nation in free throw shooting with a .763 percentage during the 1991-92 season?

 65 On December 19, 1989, eight Kentucky players did what in one game?

 66 What school has the longest current streak of consecutive winning seasons, at 48 through the 1996-97 season?

53 Danny Ferry, with 58 points

54 Gary Bradds, with 49 points

55 Oscar Robertson, with 62 points

56 Joe Scott, with 46 points

57 The University of Iowa

58 North Carolina, Kentucky, Kansas

59 Loyola of Chicago

60 Tulsa

61 The University of San Francisco

62 The University of Kentucky, on January 13, 1969

63 Notre Dame's, who beat them 71-70 during the 1973-74 season

64 Northwestern

65 Made three-point field goals

66 The University of California-Los Angeles

Danny Ferry

67 Of the top twelve winningest schools in college basketball history, which one has played the least number of seasons?

 68 Four teams have both won and lost 1,000 games in their history. Which one has a losing record?

 69 Between 1989 and 1992, what NCAA school became the first to lead the nation in scoring defense for four straight years?

 70 What was the first team in NCAA history to play forty games in a season?

 71 What team stopped San Francisco's 29-game winning streak on March 5, 1977?

 72 Arizona set the record for most fouls in a game on January 26, 1953, against Northern Arizona. How many fouls did they commit, 40, 50, or 60?

 73 What team did Loyola Marymount score their NCAA tournament record 149 points against?

 74 Indiana's 57-game winning streak was broken by what Ohio team in 1977?

 75 What school scored 150 points in a game in 1989 and lost?

 76 What school came within 3 points of scoring 100 points in a half while playing U.S. International in 1989?

 77 What school holds the NCAA record with 129 consecutive home court wins?

 78 What school ended Kentucky's NCAA record 129-game home-court winning streak?

 79 What school lost a NCAA record 37 consecutive games between 1954 and 1955?

 80 What team holds the NCAA record for most consecutive 20-win seasons?

67 North Carolina

68 Dartmouth

69 Princeton

70 Duke, in 1986

71 Notre Dame beat San Francisco 93-82

72 50

73 Michigan, in 1990

74 Toledo beat Indiana 59-57

75 U.S. International, which set a NCAA record of most points scored by a losing team

76 Oklahoma

77 Kentucky

78 Georgia Tech, beat Kentucky 59-58 in Memorial Coliseum, on January 8, 1955

79 The Citadel

80 North Carolina, at 27 and counting.

81 What university has had the most players inducted into the Naismith Memorial Basketball Hall of Fame?

 82 Who became the all-time leading scorer in Kansas University men's basketball history in 1987?

 83 Who set the record for most points scored in a men's NCAA title game in 1973?

 84 Who set the men's NCAA Final Four single game scoring record in a consolation game in 1965?

 85 What sharp-shooting Purdue Boilermaker set a record for most field goals attempted in a NCAA championship game?

 86 What school holds the NCAA record of 49 consecutive winning seasons?

 87 What player still holds rebounding records in a game, in a season, and in a career at the University of San Francisco?

 88 Only six players averaged more than 20 points a game and 20 rebounds a game during a career. Can you name one of them?

 89 Furman's Frank Selvy became the first and only Division I player in college history to do this. What did he do?

 90 What player holds the highest scoring average (minimum of six games) in NCAA tournament play at 41.3 points per game?

 91 What two players have led the nation in scoring for three straight years?

 92 What Wichita State player was the first to lead the country in scoring and in rebounding in the same season?

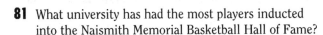 **93** What team lost more games than any other team in a season and still won the national championship?

81   Kansas, with five; Chicago University is in second place, with three

82   Danny Manning surpassed Clyde Lovellette as the all-time scoring leader at Kansas during his junior year.

83   Bill Walton scored 44 points on 21 of 22 shooting as UCLA defeated Memphis State by a score of 87 - 66.

84   Bill Bradley of Princeton scored 58 points against Wichita State in a winning cause.

85   Rick Mount, who made only 12 of the 36 shots he attempted against UCLA in 1969.

86   From 1949 through 1997, UCLA had a winning season every year.

87   Bill Russell

88   Walter Dukes, Bill Russell, Julius Erving, Paul Silas, Artis Gilmore, and Kermit Washington

89   He scored 100 points in a single game as Furman defeated Newberry on February 13, 1954. He made 41 field goals and 18 free throws. By the way, the game did not go into overtime.

90   Austin Carr, of Notre Dame

91   Pete Maravich, of Louisiana State (1968-1970) and Oscar Robertson, of Cincinnati (1958-1960)

92   Xavier McDaniel averaged 27.2 points per game and 14.8 rebounds per game in 1984-1985 in leading the nation in both categories.

93   The University of Kansas lost 11 games but won the national championship in 1988.

Clyde Lovellette

94 What player holds or shares 32 Naval Academy records?

 95 What school defeated Ole Miss 56-49 on February 19, 1982, to become the first college to record 1,300 career victories?

 96 What teams played before 54,321 people, the largest regular-season crowd in collegiate history, on January 28, 1989, at the New Orleans Superdome?

 97 What two teams began the 1991 season tied with the most collegiate career victories at 1,479 each?

 98 What UCLA player was named the MOP of the NCAA tournament in 1975?

 99 What is the only school to have the national scoring leader for four straight years?

 100 What is a triple double?

 101 Who set the record for most points in a Final Four semifinal in 1981?

 102 What team set the NCAA tournament record low of only 20 points scored in game?

 103 What former Big Eight school set the NCAA record for field goal percentage in a season by hitting 57.2 percent of their attempts in 1980?

 104 Who was the first player to end his college career with averages of over 20 points and 20 rebounds per game?

 105 Who set a record with 87 points in the 1965 Final Four?

 106 Who committed a record 17 turnovers in the 1979 NCAA tournament semifinals?

 107 Who was the first player to score 1,000 points in a season for a Division I team?

94 David Robinson

95 Kentucky

96 Louisiana State and Georgetown

97 Kentucky and North Carolina

98 Richard Washington, who scored 26 points against Louisville in the semifinals and 28 points against Kentucky in the final.

99 Furman had leading scorers Frank Selvy, in 1953 and 1954, and Darrel Floyd, in 1955 and 1956.

100 Registering double-digit figures in three different categories – scoring, rebounding, and assists – during a game.

101 Al Wood, of North Carolina, scored 39 points against Virginia in 1981.

102 North Carolina, who lost to Pittsburgh 26-20 in 1941

103 The University of Missouri

104 Walter Dukes, of Seton Hall, in 1952 - 53 (23.5 points and 21.1 rebounds)

105 Bill Bradley, of Princeton

106 Larry Bird, of Indiana State

107 Johnny O'Brien, of Seattle, in 1952

CHAPTER 9
PLAYERS

 1 Nolan Richardson scored 1,045 points for what team from 1960 through 1962?

 2 Former Boston Celtics coach Chris Ford played all forty minutes in the 1971 NCAA championship game for what team?

 3 Where did Tom Penders play college basketball?

 4 What Dayton Flyer outscored UCLA's Lew Alcindor by one point in the 1967 NCAA championship game?

 5 Who was named the Most Outstanding Player of the 1988 NCAA tournament?

 6 What player led Oklahoma A&M to back-to-back titles in 1945 and 1946?

 7 Who passed Fred Marberry to become the all-time leading scorer at Illinois State University in 1973?

 8 Who became the all-time leading scorer at Niagara University in 1970?

 9 What Houston player scored 39 points to help end UCLA's 47-game winning streak in 1968?

 10 Who was the only player to lead the nation in scoring and play for a NCAA champion in the same year?

 11 Name three players who have scored 40 points or more for Duke University in a single game.

 12 In 1989, what Iowa Hawkeye became the school's all-time leading scorer?

 13 At what school did Spencer Haywood play basketball?

1 Texas-El Paso

2 Villanova

3 Connecticut

4 Don May

5 Danny Manning, of Kansas

6 Bob Kurland

7 Doug Collins who became an Olympic and NBA star and a coach in the NBA

8 Calvin Murphy, although standing only 5' 9" tall, became an All-American and great NBA player.

9 Elvin Hayes

10 Clyde Lovelette, of Kansas, in 1952

11 Danny Ferry, Dick Groat, Jeff Mullins, Tate Armstrong, Bob Verga, Art Heyman

12 Roy Marble

13 The University of Detroit

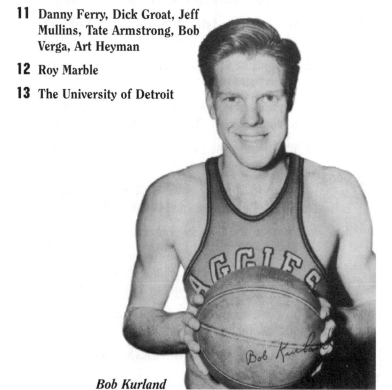

Bob Kurland

14 Who became the all-time leading scorer at Kansas State University in 1978?

 15 Who became the all-time leading scorer at Indiana University in 1987?

 16 Who passed Bill Buntin in 1970 to become the all-time leading rebounder at the University of Michigan?

 17 Name two of the top four all-time leading scorers at the University of Missouri.

 18 Who became the all-time leading scorer for the Temple Owls with 2,609 points in 1991?

 19 As of 1993, where did Wilt Chamberlain rank among the leading scorers at the University of Kansas? Was he first, fourth, eleventh, or fifteenth?

 20 Who became the all-time leading rebounder for the Georgetown Hoyas in 1985?

 21 What player became the all-time leading scorer at the University of Pittsburgh, with 2,045 points, in 1988?

 22 From 1958 to 1962, what two players won the UPI college basketball Player of the Year? They are both from the same state but not from the same school.

 23 Who was the UPI Player of the Year in 1984?

 24 Who was the UPI 1991 college basketball Player of the Year?

 25 What player became the all-time leading scorer at Princeton in 1965?

 26 Who is the all-time leading scorer at Oregon State University?

27 In 1987, Kevin Johnson became the career leader in points at what university?

14 Mike Evans, with 2,115 points

15 Steve Alford, with 2,438 points

16 Rudy Tomjanovich, with 1,039

17 Derrick Chievous, Doug Smith, Anthony Peeler, and Steve Stepanovich

18 Mark Macon

19 Eleventh remember he only played two years before joining the Harlem Globetrotters

20 Patrick Ewing

21 Charles Smith

22 Jerry Lucas, of Ohio State, and Oscar Robertson, of Cincinnati

23 Michael Jordan of the University of North Carolina

24 Shaquille O'Neal

25 Bill Bradley

26 Gary Payton, with 2,172 points

27 The University of California

Oscar Robertson

28 Richie Guerin had a sensational NBA pro career becoming the first NBA guard to score 2,000 points in a season. Where did he play college basketball?

29 Who was the 1992-93 Sports Illustrated College Basketball Rookie of the Year?

30 Mitch Richmond and Rolando Blackmon both played college basketball at what university?

31 Reggie Lewis played at what university?

32 Jeff Malone and six-time NBA All-Star Bailey Howell played at what university?

33 What player earned the Southwest Conference Player of the Decade honors for the 1970s?

34 At what university did the great Bob Pettit play?

35 What guard became the all-time leading scorer at Purdue University in 1970?

36 What player became the all-time leading scorer at Indiana State University in 1979?

37 NBA All-Star Dennis Johnson, who starred with the Seattle Supersonics, Phoenix Suns, and Boston Celtics, attended what university?

38 At what university did Rick Barry play?

39 Who became the all-time leading scorer at the University of San Francisco in 1979?

40 In 1980, Kurt Rambis became the all-time leading scorer, with 1,735 points, at what university?

41 Gene Phillips, John Koncak, and Jim Krebs are three of the all-time leading scorers at what school?

28 Iona College

29 George Washington's 7-foot 1-inch center, Yinka Dare

30 Kansas State University

31 Northeastern

32 Mississippi State

33 Otis Birdsong, of the University of Houston

34 Louisiana State University

35 Rick Mount, with 2,323 points

36 Larry Bird

37 Pepperdine University

38 The University of Miami (Florida)

39 Bill Cartwright, with 2,116 points

40 Santa Clara University

41 Southern Methodist University

42 What college did Rex Chapman attend?

 43 Dan Issel is the all-time leading scorer at what university?

 44 Who is generally thought of as leaving a lasting imprint on basketball with his one-handed "off-the-ear" shots?

 45 Maurice Stokes played at what university?

 46 The University of Seattle's 5'9" Johnny O'Brien became the first player to do what in one season?

 47 Matt Bullard, Jay Humphries, Scott Wedman, and Cliff Meely all played at what university?

 48 Pete Maravich is the SEC's all-time leading scorer with 3,667 points. In 1992-93, who became the second-leading SEC scorer?

 49 How many seasons did Larry Bird play at Indiana State?

 50 What number did Bill Walton wear at UCLA?

 51 How many seasons did Lew Alcindor play basketball at UCLA?

 52 Who is the all-time leading scorer at UCLA?

 53 Who had more rebounds at UCLA, Bill Walton or Lew Alcindor?

 54 What university did Wes Unseld attend?

42 The University of Kentucky. He left early to join the NBA.

43 The University of Kentucky

44 Stanford's Hank Luisetti

45 St. Francis College

46 He was the first player to score more than 1,000 points in one season, with 1,051 points.

47 The University of Colorado

48 Allan Houston, of Tennessee, finished his career with 2,801 points.

49 Three, 1976 through 1979

50 32

51 Four, one season on the freshman team and three as a varsity player.

52 In 1992, Don MacLean surpassed Lew Alcindor, with 2,608 points.

53 Bill Walton had three more rebounds than Alcindor, with 1,370

54 The University of Louisville

Bill Walton

55 Who was the 1993 Player of the Year in the Pac-10?

 56 Who was the 1993 Freshman of the Year in the Pac-10?

 57 Who was the NCAA tournament's Most Outstanding Player in 1986?

 58 What university did Kevin Duckworth attend?

 59 Mike Bratz was the last player to wear number 23 in Chicago before Michael Jordan claimed it. Where did Mike Bratz play college basketball?

 60 Chris Gatling, Mark West, and Kenny Gattison were all outstanding players at what university?

 61 From 1986 to 1990, what La Salle player had 115 consecutive games in which he scored in double figures?

 62 NBA great Nate Thurmond played at what university?

 63 Bob Lanier played at what university?

 64 Christian Laettner played at what school?

 65 Where did Elgin Baylor play college basketball?

 66 Johnny Dawkins played for what school?

55 Chris Mills, of the University of Arizona

56 Jason Kidd, of California

57 Pervis Ellison, of Louisville

58 Eastern Illinois University

59 Stanford

60 Old Dominion

61 Lionel Simmons

62 Bowling Green

63 St. Bonaventure

64 Duke

65 Seattle

66 Duke

Pervis Ellison

3-PT **67** Marshall Rogers, who led the nation in scoring in 1976 for Pan American University, started his career at what college?

3-PT **68** NBA players Alton Lister and Byron Scott both played at what university?

2-PT **69** At what school did Hank Gathers play?

3-PT **70** At what school did the 1963 rebound champion Paul Silas play?

3-PT **71** Kermit Washington was the NCAA rebound champion in 1972 and 1973. At what school did Kermit Washington play?

2-PT **72** What Portland State player had 71 points in a game in 1977, and 81 in a game in 1978?

3-PT **73** Who was the first player to score 50 points in a regular season game?

3-PT **74** Four St. Francis College of Pennsylvania players have played in the NBA. Name one.

2-PT **75** Fennis Dembo became the all-time leading scorer at what university in 1988?

3-PT **76** Paul Silas, Benoit Benjamin, and the great baseball pitcher Bob Gibson all played basketball at what university?

2-PT **77** The University of Georgia has retired only one jersey, number 21. Whose was it?

2-PT **78** Larry Johnson played at what university?

2-PT **79** At what school did Sean Elliott play?

2-PT **80** Julius Erving played at what university?

67 The University of Kansas

68 Arizona State

69 Loyola Marymount

70 Creighton University

71 American University

72 Freeman Williams

73 Hank Luisetti, Stanford

74 Maurice Stokes, Norm Van Lier, Kevin Porter, and Mike Iuzzolino

75 Wyoming

76 Creighton University which is located in Omaha, Nebraska

77 Dominique Wilkins

78 University of Nevada-Las Vegas (UNLV)

79 Arizona

80 Massachusetts

Sean Elliot

81 In 1953, B. H. Born became the first player from a runner-up to win the MOP award in the NCAA tournament. For what school did Born play?

 82 In 1958, what player became the first sophomore in history to win the NCAA scoring championship?

 83 Who was the only collegiate star on the Dream Team the U.S. sent to the 1992 Olympics?

 84 Who were the starting guards for the Indiana team that won the national championship over Michigan in 1976?

 85 Who were the starting guards for the 1974 North Carolina State team that defeated Marquette in the NCAA championship?

 86 Who played in the 1968 NCAA title game for North Carolina, was commissioner of the Big Ten and chairman of the Division I Men's Basketball Committee?

 87 Who made the first three-point field goal for North Carolina?

 88 Who shot the ball which was tipped in by Lorenzo Charles in North Carolina State's stunning upset of Houston in the 1983 NCAA title game?

 89 Who were the starting forwards on Ohio State's 1960 national championship team?

 90 What player scored more than 30,000 points in his NBA career yet never played in the NCAA tournament?

 91 Who was the first player to become the NBA MVP yet never compete in the NCAA tournament?

 92 Who is the first player with a single-digit regular season scoring average to score 25 points in a NCAA championship game?

81 Kansas

82 Oscar Robertson

83 Christian Laettner, of Duke

84 Quinn Buckner and Bobby Wilkerson

85 Mo Rivers and Monte Towe

86 Jim Delany

87 Matt Doherty

88 Dereck Whittenberg

89 John Havlicek and Joe Roberts

90 Julius Erving

91 Julius Erving

92 Kenny Washington, of UCLA, in 1964

Monte Towe

93 Who was the first to rank among the top five in scoring average in both the NCAA tournament and the NBA playoffs?

 94 Who was the first player to score at least 25 points in eight consecutive NCAA tournament games?

 95 Who was the first individual to be named both the NCAA's Final Four Most Outstanding Player and the NIT's Most Valuable Player?

 96 Who was the only freshman to score more than 30 points in the national semifinal or championship game?

 97 Who was the first player to twice lead the nation in scoring average while playing on teams that went to the Final Four?

 98 Who was the first major college player to score more than 21,000 points in the NBA after never participating in either the NIT or NCAA tournament?

 99 Who was the first individual to play for two NCAA champions, play for more than two NBA champions, and coach two NBA champions?

 100 Who was the first player to win the NBA Rookie of the Year and Most Valuable Player awards yet had not won any of the NCAA tournament games in which he participated?

 101 Who was the youngest player to ever play in a NCAA championship game?

 102 Who was the first guard to score more than 35 points in an NCAA title game?

 103 Who was the first junior college transfer to later be named the Final Four's Most Outstanding Player?

 104 At what university did Chuck Connors, later known as the Rifleman, play basketball?

93 Jerry West, of West Virginia and the Los Angeles Lakers.

94 Jerry West, of West Virginia

95 Tom Gola, of La Salle

96 Mike O'Koren, of North Carolina, scored 31 points in the national semifinal in 1977.

97 Oscar Robertson, of Cincinnati, 1959 and 1960. He averaged 32.6 points in 1959 and 33.7 in 1960.

98 Robert Parish, of Centenary

99 Bill Russell played for the University of San Francisco and played for and coached the Boston Celtics

100 Dave Cowens, of Florida State

101 Dolph Schayes, of New York University, was 16 when he played in the 1945 championship game

102 Gail Goodrich, of the University of California-Los Angeles, scored 42 points in 1965

103 Keith Smart, of Indiana, in 1987

104 Seton Hall